Kindness For Life

Raising Kind Children Who
Become Kind Adults Who Build
a Kinder World

Charlie Lyons

© Copyright 2024 Charles J. Lyons - All rights reserved.

The content contained within this book may not be reproduced, duplicated or transmitted without direct written permission from the author or the publisher.

Under no circumstances will any blame or legal responsibility be held against the publisher, or author, for any damages, reparation, or monetary loss due to the information contained within this book, either directly or indirectly.

Legal Notice:

This book is copyright protected. It is only for personal use. You cannot amend, distribute, sell, use, quote or paraphrase any part, or the content within this book, without the consent of the author or publisher.

Disclaimer Notice:

Please note the information contained within this document is for educational and entertainment purposes only. All effort has been executed to present accurate, up to date, reliable, complete information. No warranties of any kind are declared or implied. Readers acknowledge that the author is not engaged in the rendering of legal, financial, medical or professional advice. The content within this book has been derived from various sources. Please consult a licensed professional before attempting any techniques outlined in this book.

By reading this document, the reader agrees that under no circumstances is the author responsible for any losses, direct or indirect, that are incurred as a result of the use of the information contained within this document, including, but not limited to, errors, omissions, or inaccuracies.

Table of Contents

INTRODUCTION 1
   KINDNESS FOR LIFE DEFINED 1
   WHY RAISING KIND CHILDREN MATTERS 2
   KINDNESS IS MORE THAN JUST A VIRTUE 3
   THE RIPPLE EFFECT OF KINDNESS 4
   KINDNESS FOR LIFE: FROM MESSAGE TO MOVEMENT 6
   LET'S GO TOGETHER 8

CHAPTER 1: LEADING BY EXAMPLE 11
   THE MIRROR OF BEHAVIOR 11
   SCIENCE OF IMITATION 12
   DAILY ACTS OF KINDNESS 13
   COMPASSIONATE PROJECTS 15
   LEARNING FROM FAUX PAS 16
   ILLUSTRATIVE STORIES 17
      The Johnson Family 18
      The Patel Family 18
      The Kim Family 18
   PRACTICAL TIPS 19
   REFLECTIVE CONCLUSION 21

CHAPTER 2: CREATING A KINDNESS-FOCUSED ENVIRONMENT 23
   SETTING CLEAR EXPECTATIONS FOR KIND BEHAVIOR 23
      Understanding Kindness 24
      Tailoring Expectations to Developmental Stages 24
      Role Modeling: The Power of Example 24
      Establishing Visual and Verbal Reminders 25
      Consistency is Key 25
      Incorporating Kindness into Daily Routines 26
      Navigating Challenges with Kindness 26
      Fostering Open Communication 26
      Celebrating Successes 27

The Role of Community 27
Continuous Learning and Adaptation 27
ENCOURAGING POSITIVE INTERACTIONS WITH OTHERS 28
Specific Praise for Acts of Kindness 28
FOSTERING DIVERSE INTERACTIONS 29
Creating Opportunities for Diverse Encounters 29
Encouraging Questions and Curiosity 29
COLLABORATION OVER COMPETITION 30
Activities That Encourage Working Together 30
Family Projects and Volunteer Work 30
STRATEGIES FOR POSITIVE REINFORCEMENT AND ENCOURAGING DIVERSITY
.... 31
REFLECTING ON THE IMPACT 32
PRACTICING GRATITUDE AND APPRECIATION 33
Integrating Gratitude into Daily Routines 33
The Impact of Recognizing Kindness 34
Psychological Benefits of Gratitude 35
DESIGNING SPACES FOR KINDNESS 36
ILLUSTRATIVE STORIES 39
PRACTICAL TIPS 42
REFLECTIVE CONCLUSION 43

CHAPTER 3: FOSTERING KINDNESS THROUGH COMMUNICATION 45

OPEN AND HONEST CONVERSATIONS ABOUT KINDNESS 48
The Foundation of Kindness in Conversation 48
Initiating Conversations About Kindness 49
Through Stories and Media 49
Reflecting on Daily Interactions 49
Sharing Personal Experiences 50
The Value of Honesty and Openness 50
Encouraging Empathy and Understanding 51
Navigating Challenges with Kindness 51
Practical Applications of Kindness 51
TEACHING CONFLICT RESOLUTION SKILLS 52
The Foundation of Empathy and Respect 52
Using "I" Statements 52

Finding Compromise 53
Steps for Resolving Disagreements 53
AGE-APPROPRIATE CONFLICT SCENARIOS 54
Scenario 1: Sharing Toys (Ages 4-7) 54
Scenario 2: Group Projects (Ages 8-12) 55
Scenario 3: Social Media Misunderstandings (Ages 13-18) 55
REINFORCING KINDNESS IN CONFLICT RESOLUTION 56
EMPHASIZING TONE AND DELIVERY IN COMMUNICATION 57
The Power of Tone 57
Teaching the Impact of Tone 58
The Significance of Body Language 58
Exploring Body Language with Children 58
Choosing Words Wisely 59
Exercises in Word Choice 59
Modeling Positive Communication Habits 60
Demonstrating Kindness in Communication 60
ILLUSTRATIVE STORIES 60
The Apology that Mended Fences 61
The Lesson in Listening 62
The Bridge of Words 63
Lessons Learned 63
PRACTICAL TIPS 64
For Young Children (Ages 3-7) 65
For School-Aged Children (Ages 8-12) 66
For Teenagers (Ages 13-18) 66
For Parents and Caregivers 67
Across All Stages of Family Life 68
REFLECTIVE CONCLUSION 69

CHAPTER 4: NURTURING EMPATHY AND COMPASSION IN CHILDREN 73

TEACHING CHILDREN TO RECOGNIZE AND UNDERSTAND EMOTIONS 75
The Importance of Emotional Literacy 76
Strategies for Teaching Emotional Literacy 76
The Role of Parents in Emotional Education 77
Encouraging Perspective and Empathy 79

Role-playing Games 79
Discussing Characters' Feelings in Stories 80
Imagining Others' Perspectives 80
Emotion Guessing Games 81
Frequent, Open Discussions About Emotions and Viewpoints 81
The Empathy Jar 82
ENCOURAGING ACTS OF KINDNESS TOWARD OTHERS 82
The Importance of Kindness in Daily Life 83
Setting Kindness Goals 83
Keeping a Kindness Journal 84
Incorporating Kindness into Daily Routines 84
Examples of Simple Acts of Kindness 85
The Collective Impact of Kindness 86
ILLUSTRATIVE STORIES 86
The Lemonade Stand for a Cause 87
The Birthday Gift of Giving 87
The New Student Ambassador 88
REFLECTIVE CONCLUSION 89

CHAPTER 5: HANDLING CHALLENGES AND SETBACKS WITH KINDNESS 93

TEACHING RESILIENCE THROUGH KINDNESS 96
Modeling Resilience in Everyday Life 96
The Importance of Self-Kindness 97
Strategies for Encouraging Resilience Through Kindness .. 98
KINDNESS IN CONFLICT RESOLUTION 100
The Foundation: Empathy and Compassionate Communication 100
General Script for Compassionate Communication: 101
Techniques for De-escalating Tension 101
Finding Win-Win Solutions 102
Emphasizing Empathy in Understanding All Sides 103
SPECIFIC SCRIPTS FOR COMPASSIONATE COMMUNICATION 104
Young Children (Ages 3 to 7) 104
School-aged children (Ages 8-12) 107
Teenagers (Ages 13-17) 111

LEARNING FROM MISTAKES WITH A KIND HEART 114
REFLECTIVE CONCLUSION 117

CHAPTER 6: CULTIVATING A KINDNESS MINDSET FOR LIFE ...119

THE KINDNESS MINDSET 119
What is a Kindness Mindset? 120
The Significance of a Kindness Mindset 120
Influence on Decision-Making and Relationships 121
Psychological Research and Expert Opinions 121
The Kindness Mindset as a Gift and Responsibility 122
DAILY PRACTICES 123
Starting the Day with Kind Intentions 124
Recognizing Opportunities for Kindness in Everyday Moments 124
Ending the Day with Reflection on Kind Acts 125
Adapting Practices for Different Ages and Stages of Development 126
POSITIVE REINFORCEMENT 127
The Role of Praise in Reinforcing Kindness 127
Balancing Praise and Rewards 128
Encouraging a Kindness Mindset Beyond Acts 129
KINDNESS AS A FAMILY VALUE 131
Establishing Kindness as a Core Family Value 131
Celebrating Kindness in Daily Life 132
Embedding Kindness Through Rituals and Traditions 132
Strategies for Sustaining Kindness as a Family Value 133
PRACTICAL TIPS 134
Dealing with Unkind Behavior 135
Navigating Societal Pressures 136
Building Resilience in Kindness 137
Maintaining a Kindness Mindset 138
REFLECTIVE CONCLUSION 139
Reflective Questions 139
Prompts for Setting Goals 140

CHAPTER 7: DIGITAL KINDNESS: NAVIGATING THE ONLINE WORLD 143

- Understanding the Impact of Cyberbullying 144
  - Defining Cyberbullying 145
  - Consequences of Cyberbullying 145
  - Prevention and Response Strategies 146
- Promoting Empathy in Digital Communications 148
  - Empathy Online 148
  - Understanding Digital Footprints 149
  - Role-Playing and Scenarios 149
- Being a Positive Influence Online 150
  - Modeling Positive Online Behavior 151
  - Creating Positive Content 151
  - Digital Citizenship 152
- Navigating Social Media and Online Interactions 153
  - Setting Boundaries 154
  - Critical Consumption of Online Content 155
  - Building a Kind Online Community 156
- The Role of Parents in Digital Kindness 157
  - Ongoing Communication 158
  - Education about Digital Literacy 158
  - Setting a Positive Example 159
  - The Journey Together 159

CHAPTER 8: EMBRACING KINDNESS AS A PARENT 161

- Self-Kindness in Parenting 161
- Navigating Parenting Challenges 163
- Building a Kindness Community 166
- Illustrative Stories 168
  - Julia's Journey to Self-Acceptance 168
  - Marcus: Finding Balance in Single Parenthood 169
  - Emma's Transformation Through Gratitude 169
  - The Power of Self-Kindness in Parenting 170
- Practical Tips 170
- Reflective Conclusion 173

CHAPTER 9: KINDNESS FOR LIFE 177

- Kindness That Lasts a Lifetime 177
- Kindness For All of Life 180

Schools: The Lunchtime Hero 180
Workplaces: The Compassionate CEO 180
Communities: The Neighborhood's Heart 181
Politics: The Diplomat of Peace 181
Between Strangers: The Chain of Coffees 182
Healthcare: The Generous Pharmacist 182
Sports: The Compassionate Coach 183
Arts and Culture: The Mural of Unity 183
Environmental Conservation: The Kindness Grove 183
Public Services: The Library of Hope 184
The Ripple Effect Revisited 185
A Personal Note 187
Passing It On 188

APPENDIX: RESOURCES FOR FURTHERING KINDNESS 191

Books 191
Parenting and Kindness 191
Empathy and Compassion 193
Personal Development 195
Websites and Online Resources 196

ABOUT THE AUTHOR 199

REFERENCES 201

To my wife and partner in parenting, Lindsey
for teaching me the value of kindness through her
unwavering love and support;

To my children, Caleb, Olivia, and Annie
who inspire me every day with their boundless
kindness and empathy;

And to all the parents
dedicated to nurturing the seeds of kindness in their
children's hearts.

Introduction

Wherever there is a human being, there is an opportunity for kindness. –Seneca

Kindness is the language which the deaf can hear and the blind can see. –Mark Twain

Three things in human life are important: the first is to be kind; the second is to be kind; and the third is to be kind.
–Henry James

Kindness For Life Defined

The quiet whisper of kindness can feel lost in the wind. Yet, kindness has the potential to transform hearts, mend bridges, and light up the darkest places.

Amid the whirlwind that often characterizes the lives of families, a profound opportunity is nestled—one that extends beyond the immediacies of daily routines and transcends the often-tumultuous phases of childhood. This opportunity is not found in pursuing academic excellence or extracurricular achievements. Instead, it lies in the heart of a concept so fundamental yet so profound that its impact echoes throughout the lifetime of an individual and, indeed, across the fabric of society itself. ***This opportunity is the chance to raise not just successful individuals but kind-hearted ones.***

Kindness For Life is not merely a call to action; it is an invitation to embark on a journey that begins within the confines of our hearts and stretches out into our communities and the vast world beyond.

Kindness For Life: Raising Kind Children Who Become Kind Adults Who Build a Kinder World embarks on a journey to underscore the importance of nurturing this quintessential virtue from the cradle onward, laying the groundwork for a society where kindness is the currency of human interaction.

Why Raising Kind Children Matters

The chaos that often defines family life, with its sleepless nights, endless laundry, and the perpetual balancing act between personal and parental responsibilities, might seem an unlikely backdrop for profound philosophical undertakings. Yet, within this chaos, the seeds of kindness can be sown. Raising kind children matters immensely because, at the heart of every societal interaction, every community engagement, and every personal relationship lies the need for empathy, understanding, and, fundamentally, kindness.

In a world increasingly marked by divisiveness and intolerance, the importance of instilling the values of kindness in the next generation cannot be overstated.

Kind-hearted individuals stand out. They illuminate paths toward mutual respect and understanding in a societal landscape clouded by conflict and discord. When we prioritize cultivating kindness in our children, we invest in a future where success is measured not just by personal achievement but by the positive impact one has on the lives of others.

Kindness Is More Than Just a Virtue

To conceive of kindness merely as a virtue is to underestimate its transformative power. Kindness is the cornerstone of healthy, enduring relationships and the bedrock of a thriving society. When children learn the value of kindness, they are equipped with a compass for navigating the complexities of human interaction. They learn to see the world through the eyes of others, to embrace diversity with open arms, and to respond to challenges with empathy and understanding.

More than an inherent trait, kindness is a skill that can be nurtured, cultivated, and refined through practice. By providing our children with daily opportunities to express kindness, we empower them to become agents of positive change. Much research underscores this approach's myriad benefits: kind children tend to be happier, more resilient, and better equipped to face adversity. They forge stronger relationships, exhibit higher levels of emotional intelligence, and enjoy a sense of fulfillment from meaningful engagement with the world around them.

Kindness is the foundation upon which a life of significance and contentment is built. (We'll highlight some of these specific studies a little later.)

The Ripple Effect of Kindness

Perhaps the most compelling reason to prioritize kindness in our parenting journey is the potential for a profound and far-reaching ripple effect. This concept, illustrated by the image of a pebble thrown into a still pond, captures how acts of kindness can extend well beyond their initial point of impact. Each act of kindness, whether small or seemingly insignificant, sets off a cascade of positive effects that ripple outward, touching lives and hearts in ways we might never fully comprehend.

When we raise kind children, we essentially cast pebbles into society's vast pond. Through their acts of kindness, these children initiate waves of positivity that reach far and wide. A single act of kindness by a child can brighten someone's day, inspire further acts of kindness, and set a tone of generosity and compassion within their community. This ripple effect can transcend the boundaries of our immediate social circles, influencing others in distant corners of society and fostering a culture of empathy and understanding.

Moreover, the ripple effect of kindness serves to knit the fabric of our communities more tightly together. In a society where individualism prevails, acts of kindness remind us of the interconnectedness of our lives. They demonstrate that our actions, no matter how small, have the power to affect others profoundly. This interconnectedness fostered through kindness creates a stronger, more resilient community capable of facing challenges with unity and grace.

The ripple effect also has a transformative impact on the individuals who practice kindness. Children who learn the value of kindness and see the effect of their actions develop a sense of agency and responsibility toward others. They grow in the understanding that they have the power to make a positive difference in the world, one act of kindness at a time. This realization empowers them, boosts their self-esteem, and fosters a sense of purpose.

Furthermore, the ripple effect of kindness reinforces the concept of reciprocity. In a world where kindness has become the norm, children grow up in environments where they are more likely to receive kindness in return. This creates a virtuous cycle, where acts of kindness are given and received, amplifying the overall sense of well-being and happiness within communities.

Emphasizing the ripple effect of kindness, it's crucial to recognize that every act of kindness, no matter how small, is part of a larger narrative of positive change. This is a testament to the power of individual actions to contribute to a collective impact. As parents, caregivers, and community members, we have the unique opportunity to model and encourage this behavior, setting in motion waves of kindness that can transform our world.

By nurturing kind children, we raise individuals equipped to face the world with empathy and compassion and plant the seeds for a more compassionate and inclusive society—a world where empathy reigns supreme and differences are celebrated rather than feared.

Through the ripple effect of kindness, we can envision a future where each act of kindness begets another, creating an endless wave of positivity that reshapes the world for the better.

Kindness For Life: From Message to Movement

The book's title, *Kindness For Life*, carries a beautiful double entendre. On one level, it suggests that kindness is a lifelong commitment to be nurtured and practiced throughout one's life. On another level, it implies that kindness enriches life, enhancing the quality and experience of living for both the giver and the receiver.

With this dual meaning, I invite you to consider the enduring nature of kindness and its transformative power in your life and the lives of others. I hope this message conveys both a method of living and the benefits that come from such a lifestyle. Kindness lasts a lifetime and infuses life with unparalleled purpose and joy.

The message is evident in a world that often seems overrun with critics and cynicism: We need more kindness. I frequently recite this phrase in my life and work: *"The world has too many critics. We need more kindness. Pass it on."* Until I started writing this book, I had always thought of this in terms of kindness as a message that goes from one person to another. However, we need kindness to be far more than a message; we need it to be a movement. Movements begin when one person rallies a small group, which gets bigger and bigger until, suddenly (in today's language), the message goes viral.

Let me give you some high-level housekeeping stuff before we get going.

I'm a big believer in *rubber meets the road* learning, so right out of the gate, in chapter one, I provide some concrete practicalities of the principles we'll discuss. Every chapter has a list or two of practical tips for living out what you're learning. It's important to note that there are a lot of tips and strategies in this book—too many for any family to implement at any one time. So, based on the season of life, your family background, or even basic inclinations, it's probably best for you and your family to identify and implement two or three strategies at a time. Maybe make it an annual goal to take on one or two more significant areas of concern for your household. Overall, please keep it simple.

Additionally, most chapters conclude with a handful of reflection questions to help you home in on some adjustments you can make personally to apply what you learn immediately. These are essential checkpoints along the journey; don't skim over them!

Let's Go Together

I'm a big advocate for learning from older mentors, the 'gray-haired heroes' of parenting, who have journeyed through all stages of child-rearing—I've read many of their books, and you probably have, too. There are lessons learned from them here in these pages. However, I also firmly believe there's much to be learned from peers who are 'in the trenches' alongside me. That's the approach I'm taking here with *Kindness For Life*. I've learned and applied some of the things I'm passing along from others in a similar season of life who are walking the parenting journey alongside my wife and me.

I'm glad you're along as we navigate the rewarding, albeit challenging, journey of parenting with kindness at its core. Together, we can lay the groundwork for a future where kindness is not just a temporary aspiration that goes viral but a reality that gets passed on and lasts for generations—a reality that begins with us, here and now.

The call to action is evident at the threshold of this journey: to embrace the opportunity to raise kind children with intentionality and purpose. Let's commit to being examples of kindness in our lives, knowing that ***every act of kindness, no matter how small, contributes to a more significant wave of positive change.*** This book is an invitation to join a movement toward a world where kindness defines the essence of human interaction.

Raising kind children who become kind adults is one of the most significant legacies we can leave behind us. It's a journey fraught with challenges but abounding with rewards. As you turn the following pages, let them serve as a roadmap for this journey, guiding you through the practicalities, strategies, and heart-warming rewards of raising children who embody the true spirit of kindness.

Let's make kindness our guide, goal, and gift to future generations for our children's growth, our communities' health, and our world's future.

Friends, the world has too many critics.

We need more kindness.

Pass it on.

Chapter 1:
Leading by Example

Children have never been very good at listening to their elders, but they have never failed to imitate them. –James Baldwin

Children learn more from what you are than what you teach.
–W.E.B. Du Bois

Example is not the main thing in influencing others. It is the only thing. –Albert Schweitzer

The Mirror of Behavior

Imagine a Saturday morning at the local coffee shop: a parent and their child are in line, waiting to order. The parent, noticing the barista looks worn out, offers a warm smile and asks how their day is going, genuinely listening to the response. They then pay for the coffee of the person standing behind them, turning to their child to explain, "It's nice to make someone's day brighter, don't you think?" The child, absorbing every action and every word, nods, and their eyes alight with the spark of newfound understanding. This simple interaction sets a powerful example: kindness is not just a concept to be discussed but a practice to be lived. As parents, our behavior is a mirror in which our children see their reflection. Through our actions, we teach them the language of kindness, showing them how to navigate the world with empathy and grace. This narrative is a gentle reminder that every act of kindness, no matter how small, is a step toward shaping a kinder, more compassionate future.

Science of Imitation

The inclination of children to mimic the adults in their lives is a well-documented phenomenon in developmental psychology. This imitation goes beyond simple mimicry; it is a fundamental part of the learning process, enabling children to acquire new skills, understand social norms, and develop empathy. The theory of social learning, pioneered by Albert Bandura, posits that children learn social behavior primarily through observing and imitating others, especially those they consider role models. Bandura's research showed that children are more likely to imitate rewarded behaviors or those they see, leading to positive outcomes for the imitator (Bandura, 1969).

This psychological foundation underscores the critical role parents play in modeling kindness. When children witness acts of kindness, compassion, and empathy from their parents, these behaviors become ingrained in their psyche as desirable and normative. They learn not only the acts themselves but also the underlying values that motivate these actions. The emotional responses reinforce this learning process these acts elicit—both in themselves and others—strengthening their understanding of kindness's social and emotional significance. The old leadership proverb is that *more is caught than taught.*

Furthermore, mirror neurons, a discovery that revolutionized our understanding of social learning, play a pivotal role in this process. These neurons fire when an individual acts and when they observe the same action performed by another (Iacoboni, 2009). This mirroring mechanism enables children to not only copy behaviors but also empathize with the emotional states of others. Through this neurological foundation, children develop the capacity for empathy, a cornerstone of kindness.

These insights have profound implications for parenting. They suggest that every interaction, gesture of kindness, or moment of empathy is a teaching opportunity. By consciously modeling positive behavior, parents can foster an environment where kindness and compassion are taught and lived. This environment encourages children to internalize these values, shaping their understanding and practice of kindness throughout their lives.

Daily Acts of Kindness

Kindness can be woven into the fabric of daily life through simple, intentional acts. Here are specific acts of kindness parents can perform, showcasing the variety and consistency vital to embedding these values:

1. **Greet Everyone Warmly**: Start each day by greeting your family members with warmth and affection. A good morning hug or a cheerful hello sets a positive tone for the day.

2. **Express Gratitude**: Make it a habit to express gratitude for the little things. Thank your child for helping around the house or for their patience while running errands.

3. **Compliment Generously**: Offer genuine compliments to family members, friends, and strangers. Acknowledge efforts, celebrate achievements, and appreciate unique qualities.

4. **Listen Actively**: Show kindness by giving your full attention during conversations. Listen to understand, not to respond, demonstrating that you value others' thoughts and feelings.

5. **Leave Kind Notes**: Surprise family members with handwritten notes of encouragement and love tucked into lunchboxes or left on pillows.

6. **Practice Patience**: Exhibit patience in moments of stress or frustration, showing children that kindness extends to how we respond to challenges.

These simple yet profound acts serve as daily reminders of the power of kindness. By incorporating them into routine interactions, parents can create a living curriculum of compassion and empathy for their children to emulate. We'll dig a little deeper in the following chapters.

Compassionate Projects

Engaging in compassionate projects as a family is a powerful way to implement kindness. These activities benefit the community and reinforce the value of empathy and service in children. Here's how families can plan and execute projects centered on compassion:

1. **Identifying a Need**: Begin by discussing as a family what issues or needs in the community resonate with you. Whether helping at an animal shelter, organizing a neighborhood clean-up, or supporting a local food bank, choose a project that aligns with your family's interests and values.

2. **Planning Together**: Once you've identified a project, involve everyone in the planning process. Assign tasks based on age and ability, ensuring each family member feels they have a meaningful role.

3. **Executing the Project**. During the project, emphasize teamwork and the importance of each

person's contribution. Share observations about the people you're helping and discuss the potential impact of your actions.

4. **Reflecting on the Experience**: After completing the project, reflect on the experience as a family. Discuss what you learned, how it felt to help others, and what other actions you might take in the future to continue making a difference.

By participating in compassionate projects, families contribute to the well-being of their communities and instill in their children a lifelong commitment to kindness and service.

Learning from Faux Pas

Empathy is the heartbeat of kindness—a capacity that allows us to understand and share the feelings of another. Developing empathy is crucial for children, and parents can play a pivotal role in this process by demonstrating empathy in action. We'll discuss the development of empathy in children later, but we have to recognize that it starts with us as parents and caregivers being empathetic to ourselves first.

Mistakes are inevitable, but they offer valuable learning opportunities, especially when teaching kindness and humility. Here's a story that illustrates how a parent turned a personal mistake into a teachable moment for both themselves and their child:

Sarah was running late for an appointment and, in her haste, accidentally cut off another driver. Realizing her mistake, she saw it as an opportunity to teach her son, Jake, about accountability and kindness. Once safely parked, she turned to Jake and said, "I made a mistake back there. I wasn't paying enough attention, so I cut someone off. It's important to be careful and considerate, even when we're in a hurry." Later, with Jake's help, Sarah wrote an apology note and left it on the windshield of the car she'd cut off.

This experience taught Jake several valuable lessons: the importance of acknowledging mistakes, the value of taking responsibility, and the power of a simple act of kindness to make amends. By turning her faux pas into a learning opportunity, Sarah not only reinforced the principles of kindness and humility but also demonstrated that it's never too late to do the right thing.

Illustrative Stories

In the journey of fostering kindness, every family's story is unique, yet each share a common thread—the transformative impact of parental modeling on children's understanding and practice of kindness. Here are narratives from various families showcasing how parents have successfully modeled kindness:

The Johnson Family

Mark and Linda Johnson habitually volunteered monthly with their two children at their local food bank. Through these experiences, their children learned the importance of community service and developed a deep empathy for those in need. The Johnsons' commitment to regular service taught their children that kindness is not a one-time act but a way of life.

The Patel Family

Amit and Priya Patel emphasized the importance of kindness through daily acts of gratitude. Every evening at dinner, each family member shared something they were grateful for and something kind they did for someone else that day. This routine fostered a culture of gratitude and kindness within the family and encouraged their children to look for opportunities to be kind each day.

The Kim Family

Young and Soo Kim encouraged their children to engage in "random acts of kindness" by leaving surprise notes of encouragement for neighbors and classmates. This simple yet impactful practice taught their children the joy of brightening someone else's day and the value of spreading kindness without expecting anything in return.

Through these stories, it becomes evident that modeling kindness in various ways can significantly influence children's attitudes and behaviors. Each family's approach, whether through service, gratitude, or spontaneous acts of kindness, contributes to a larger narrative of compassion and empathy.

Practical Tips

Integrating the principles of kindness into daily life can be both rewarding and challenging. Here are practical tips for parents seeking to embody and promote kindness within their families:

1. **Lead by Example**: Remember, children are always watching. Make a conscious daily effort to demonstrate kindness in your actions and words.

2. **Make Kindness a Family Value**: Discuss the importance of kindness with your children. Make it clear that being kind is a priority for your family, and explain why it matters.

3. **Recognize Kind Acts**: When you notice your child being kind, acknowledge and praise their behavior. This reinforces the value of kindness and encourages them to continue acting compassionately.

4. **Use Kindness to Resolve Conflicts**: Teach your children to use kindness and empathy to navigate disagreements. Encourage them to consider the other person's perspective and to find compassionate solutions.

5. **Incorporate Kindness into Routines**: Whether volunteering together or simply performing acts of kindness for each other, make kindness a regular part of your family's routine.

6. **Read Stories About Kindness**: Share books and stories that highlight the importance of kindness. Discuss the characters' actions and the impact their kindness had on others, encouraging your children to think about how they can be kind in their own lives.

7. **Address Unkind Behavior Appropriately**: When unkind behavior occurs, address it constructively. Discuss why the behavior was hurtful and explore alternative actions that could have been taken. This teaches children that kindness is a choice, even in difficult situations.

8. **Encourage Empathy**: Encourage your children to think about how others feel in various situations. Ask questions like, "How would you feel if that happened to you?" to foster empathy and consideration for others.

9. **Kindness Challenge**: Create a family kindness challenge in which each member tries to perform a certain number of kind acts within a week. Share your experiences and the reactions you receive, turning it into a fun and meaningful family activity.

10. **Lead with Forgiveness**: Show your children the power of forgiveness. Discuss the importance of forgiving others, not holding grudges, and moving forward with kindness and understanding.

By incorporating these practical tips into daily life, parents can help cultivate a kindness mindset in their children, setting them up for a lifetime of compassionate interactions and relationships.

Reflective Conclusion

As we conclude this chapter on leading by example, it's vital for us, as parents and caregivers, to pause and reflect on our behaviors and the example we set for our children. Raising kind children starts with us—their first and most influential role models. Every act of kindness we demonstrate, every compassionate word we speak, and every empathetic gesture we make plant seeds of kindness in our children's hearts.

This reflection is not about dwelling on our imperfections or the moments we fall short but about recognizing our power to shape the world into a kinder, more compassionate place, starting with our own families. It's about making a conscious daily decision to model the values we wish to instill in our children, knowing that our actions speak louder than our words.

As you progress from this chapter, I encourage you to embrace your role as a kindness model with intentionality and purpose. Consider the practical tips shared, the stories of families walking this path alongside you, and the profound impact your example can have on your child's understanding and practice of kindness. Remember, the journey of a thousand miles begins with a single step. Let that step be one of kindness, and let the path you pave be one your children can proudly follow.

In raising kind children who become kind adults, we're not just nurturing the next generation but contributing to a legacy of kindness that can transform the world. Let's embark on this journey with open hearts and a steadfast commitment to leading by example, for in the mirror of our behavior, our children learn the most valuable lessons of all.

Chapter 2:
Creating a Kindness-Focused Environment

Environment is the invisible hand that shapes human behavior.
—James Clear

A warm smile is the universal language of kindness.
—William Arthur Ward

No act of kindness, no matter how small, is ever wasted.
—Aesop, The Lion and the Mouse

Setting Clear Expectations for Kind Behavior

Creating a culture of kindness within the family begins with setting clear, understandable, and consistent expectations for behavior. This process is foundational to teaching children compassion, empathy, and respect for others. It involves not just verbal instructions but a comprehensive approach that integrates discussion, role modeling, and practical application into the fabric of daily family life.

Understanding Kindness

The first step in setting clear expectations is to define what kindness means in your family context. Kindness can encompass a range of behaviors, from sharing and helping others to expressing gratitude and showing empathy. It's essential to discuss with your children what kindness looks like in specific, relatable terms. For young children, kindness could be as simple as sharing toys or saying please and thank you. For older children and teenagers, it might involve more complex concepts like standing up for someone being bullied or volunteering their time to help others.

Tailoring Expectations to Developmental Stages

Expectations for kind behavior should be age-appropriate and tailored to the developmental stage of each child. Young children are learning to navigate social interactions and can start with basic acts of kindness. As children grow, these expectations can evolve to include a deeper understanding of empathy, the impact of their words and actions on others, and the importance of inclusivity and respect for diversity.

Role Modeling: The Power of Example

Children learn about kindness from direct teaching and observing the behavior of adults around them. Parents and caregivers are the most influential role models. Demonstrating kindness in your actions, speaking to others, and speaking about others when they are absent teaches children the value of kindness in all interactions. This includes showing kindness within the family, in public, and in resolving conflicts, offering a consistent model for children to emulate.

Establishing Visual and Verbal Reminders

Visual reminders, such as a family kindness chart or agreement, can help reinforce these expectations. Creating this together as a family activity can further solidify the commitment to these values. This chart might list specific behaviors considered kind, ways to support each other, and how to express gratitude and empathy daily. Regularly referring to and updating this chart keeps the concept of kindness visible and central in the home.

Consistency is Key

Maintaining consistency is one of the most challenging yet crucial aspects of parenting, and setting expectations for kind behavior is no exception. This means consistently recognizing and praising acts of kindness and constructively addressing behaviors that fall short of these expectations. It involves creating a balance where kindness is celebrated and seen as a standard, expected part of daily life.

Incorporating Kindness into Daily Routines

Making kindness a daily practice involves more than just recognizing kind acts; it's about integrating kindness into the very structure of family life. This might mean setting aside time each day to share acts of kindness each person has experienced or performed, or it could involve weekly family meetings to discuss how to help someone in need. Incorporating kindness into daily routines makes it a habit, reinforcing that being kind is part of who we are as a family.

Navigating Challenges with Kindness

Challenges will inevitably arise, and not every moment will be a perfect embodiment of kindness. Children, like adults, can have bad days, react poorly to situations, or struggle to meet set expectations. These moments provide valuable learning opportunities. Discussing these challenges openly, exploring why a particular behavior wasn't kind, and discussing how to make a better choice next time reinforce the learning process and demonstrate that kindness also involves forgiveness and growth.

Fostering Open Communication

Open, honest communication is vital in setting and maintaining expectations for kind behavior. This means talking about what behaviors are expected and why they matter. Encouraging children to express their feelings, listen to others, and resolve conflicts with kindness fosters an environment where empathy and understanding can flourish.

Celebrating Successes

While it's essential to address challenges, celebrating successes is equally important. Recognizing and praising acts of kindness, no matter how small, reinforces positive behavior and encourages more. This can be as simple as a verbal acknowledgment, a note of appreciation, or a particular family activity to celebrate acts of kindness.

The Role of Community

Extending the conversation about kindness beyond the immediate family and the broader community can reinforce the importance of these values. Participating in community service projects, attending cultural events, and engaging with diverse groups can provide practical experiences of kindness, empathy, and inclusivity.

Continuous Learning and Adaptation

Finally, setting clear expectations for kind behavior is not a one-time event but an ongoing process that evolves as children grow and learn. Regularly revisiting these expectations, discussing how they apply in new situations, and adapting them as needed ensures that the concept of kindness grows with your family.

Encouraging Positive Interactions with Others

Positive reinforcement plays a pivotal role in shaping behaviors, with its effects particularly profound in children's development of kindness and empathy. This psychological principle suggests that behaviors followed by favorable outcomes are more likely to recur. In the context of fostering kindness, this means acknowledging and rewarding acts of empathy and generosity, thereby encouraging their repetition.

Specific Praise for Acts of Kindness

The effectiveness of positive reinforcement is significantly enhanced by specificity. Rather than general commendations, specific praise acknowledges the particular act of kindness, making the positive feedback more meaningful. For instance, instead of a broad "good job," saying "I really appreciated how you helped your sister with her homework without being asked; it shows how thoughtful you are," directly ties the praise to the kind act, reinforcing the desired behavior.

Fostering Diverse Interactions

One of the rich tapestries of life is the diversity it encompasses—cultures, perspectives, and experiences. Encouraging children to interact with a wide range of individuals is crucial in developing empathy and understanding.

Creating Opportunities for Diverse Encounters

Parents can actively seek diverse environments to create opportunities for their children to engage with people from various backgrounds. This could involve participating in cultural festivals, attending workshops or classes focusing on different traditions, or simply fostering friendships with families from various cultural, racial, religious, or socioeconomic backgrounds. Such interactions enrich children's understanding of the world, teaching them to appreciate and celebrate the differences that make each person unique.

Encouraging Questions and Curiosity

Curiosity is a natural pathway to understanding. Encouraging children to ask questions and express their curiosity about different cultures and lifestyles respectfully opens the door to more profound empathy. Parents can facilitate this by modeling curiosity themselves, asking thoughtful questions, and seeking answers together with their children.

Collaboration Over Competition

While competition has its place in motivating and challenging individuals, emphasizing collaboration over competition in family activities and values can foster a more inclusive and supportive environment.

Activities That Encourage Working Together

Activities that require cooperation to achieve a common goal can teach children the value of working together. This could be as simple as a family art project where each member contributes to a larger piece or as complex as organizing a community clean-up. Games and activities focusing on team success rather than individual achievement can also reinforce the importance of supporting one another.

Family Projects and Volunteer Work

Engaging in volunteer work as a family or undertaking projects that benefit the community or environment can instill a sense of collective purpose and achievement. These activities encourage collaboration and demonstrate the impact of kindness and cooperation in real-world scenarios.

Strategies for Positive Reinforcement and Encouraging Diversity

To effectively use positive reinforcement and encourage diversity in interactions, consider the following strategies:

1. **Catch Them Being Kind**: Be on the lookout for spontaneous acts of kindness and empathy from your children, and make sure to acknowledge them immediately and specifically.

2. **Diverse Books and Media**: Introduce children to books, movies, and other media that represent a wide array of cultures, experiences, and perspectives. Discuss these stories and their characters, focusing on the values of empathy and understanding.

3. **Role-Playing Different Perspectives**: Use role-playing games to explore different scenarios from multiple perspectives. This can help children understand the feelings and viewpoints of others, fostering empathy and kindness.

4. **Family Discussion Nights**: Dedicate weekly time to discuss various topics related to kindness, empathy, diversity, and cooperation. Use this time to share experiences, address questions, and explore new ideas together.

5. **Encouragement and Rewards**: Use verbal encouragement and tangible rewards as positive reinforcement for kind behavior. This could include a kindness chart with stickers for younger children or earning special privileges for older children.

6. **Set an Example**: Children are incredibly observant, and, as already discussed, they often emulate the behavior they see. Demonstrating kindness, empathy, and a willingness to collaborate and learn from others is a powerful example for them to follow.

Reflecting on the Impact

The cumulative effect of encouraging positive interactions, emphasizing diversity, and fostering an environment of collaboration over competition cannot be overstated. These practices benefit individual children and families and contribute to a more empathetic, understanding, and cohesive society. By instilling these values early and reinforcing them through specific praise and positive reinforcement, parents can help their children develop into kind, empathetic adults who value diversity and understand the importance of working together toward common goals.

Through consistent effort, intentional planning, and an unwavering commitment, families can cultivate a culture where kindness thrives through specific praise, diverse interactions, and collaborative activities, setting the stage for a more empathetic and inclusive world.

Practicing Gratitude and Appreciation

Gratitude is a cornerstone in building a kindness-focused environment. Through gratitude, families can shift their perspective from lacking to appreciating the abundance in their lives, thus fostering a culture of kindness and generosity. This section outlines practical methods for weaving gratitude into daily family life and discusses the profound impact this practice can have on individual well-being and the collective family dynamic.

Integrating Gratitude into Daily Routines

One effective method for fostering gratitude is incorporating it into daily routines, making it as habitual as morning coffee or bedtime stories. A gratitude journal is a simple yet powerful tool for individuals of all ages. Encouraging each family member to jot down three things for which they're grateful daily can cultivate a habit of looking for the positive in every situation. These entries can then serve as a basis for reflection and discussion, strengthening family bonds and reinforcing the practice of gratitude.

Similarly, thank-you notes offer a tangible way to express appreciation for others' kindness, impacting both the giver and receiver. Encouraging children to write thank-you notes for gifts, acts of kindness, or even for everyday contributions from family members can teach them to acknowledge and appreciate the role others play in their happiness.

Another powerful practice is sharing what each family member is thankful for during family meals. This can transform mealtime into a meaningful opportunity for connection and reflection, highlighting the day's positive aspects and fostering a sense of collective gratitude.

The Impact of Recognizing Kindness

Recognizing and appreciating the kindness of others can amplify positive feelings and behaviors within the family unit and extend these positive vibes into the broader community. This reciprocal nature of gratitude encourages a cycle of kindness, where one good deed begets another, contributing to a more supportive and caring environment.

Psychological Benefits of Gratitude

The practice of gratitude is not only beneficial for nurturing a kind environment but also offers significant psychological benefits. Studies have shown that gratitude can increase overall well-being, reduce symptoms of depression, and enhance resilience in the face of adversity (Wood et el., 2010; Tomczyk et al., 2022; Kumar et al., 2022). By focusing on the positive and acknowledging the kindness of others, individuals can cultivate a more optimistic outlook on life, counteracting negativity and entitlement.

Gratitude can be a buffer against the self-centeredness that sometimes pervades modern life. By regularly acknowledging the contributions of others to our well-being, we teach our children to look beyond themselves, fostering empathy and a deep sense of interconnectedness with those around them.

Incorporating gratitude into daily routines, recognizing the kindness of others, and understanding the psychological benefits of gratitude are pivotal steps in creating a kindness-focused environment. These practices not only enrich the lives of individual family members but also weave a fabric of kindness and appreciation that extends beyond the confines of the home, impacting the broader community.

Designing Spaces for Kindness

The architecture of our lives—the spaces where we dwell, learn, and play—profoundly influences our behavior, emotions, and interactions with others. Recognizing this intrinsic link between physical environment and human behavior opens up possibilities for fostering kindness, empathy, and cooperation within our daily lives. Here, we'll take a look at how thoughtfully designed and organized spaces can serve as catalysts for cultivating a culture of kindness, transforming homes into nurturing environments that encourage positive interactions and shared experiences.

At the heart of designing spaces for kindness is the understanding that our surroundings can either facilitate or hinder our interactions with others. Spaces that are open, accessible, and versatile invite collaboration and sharing, while cramped, segregated areas may inadvertently promote isolation and self-centeredness. Thus, the deliberate organization and design of living spaces can significantly impact the development of kindness and cooperation among family members.

Consider the living room, often the heart of the home, where family members gather to relax and connect. A living room designed with kindness in mind would prioritize comfortable seating arranged to encourage face-to-face interactions, fostering open communication and shared experiences. Such a space might feature a circular or semi-circular seating arrangement around a central point, like a coffee table, creating an inviting atmosphere for conversation, board games, and other cooperative activities. This layout subtly encourages family members to engage with each other, share stories, and offer support, laying the groundwork for empathetic connections.

Moving beyond the living room, the kitchen, sometimes called the home's soul, offers another prime opportunity to design for kindness. A kitchen with an open layout that includes a communal dining area invites participation from all family members, whether in meal preparation, cooking, or cleaning up. This inclusive design facilitates shared experiences and teaches valuable lessons in cooperation and consideration for others. Preparing a meal together becomes more than just a daily task; it transforms into a collaborative endeavor that nurtures family bonds and fosters a sense of communal achievement.

Even spaces like bedrooms and bathrooms, typically considered private areas, can be thoughtfully designed to encourage kindness and sharing. For instance, siblings sharing a bedroom can benefit from a layout that respects individual space while also incorporating shared areas for joint activities, promoting both independence and cooperation. Similarly, organizing a bathroom with shared toiletries or implementing a schedule for its use can teach respect, patience, and consideration, reinforcing the importance of thinking about others' needs alongside our own.

Beyond the organization of individual rooms, the overall flow and accessibility of a home play crucial roles in promoting kindness and empathy. Creating spaces that are physically accessible to all family members, regardless of age or ability, sends a powerful message of inclusivity and care. Features such as wide doorways, ramps instead of steps, and easily accessible storage solutions make daily life more convenient and embody the principles of consideration and support central to kindness.

Moreover, outdoor spaces, whether gardens, patios, or balconies, provide unique opportunities to extend the ethos of kindness beyond the home's interior. These areas can be designed to encourage family members to engage with nature and each other, offering settings for cooperative gardening projects, outdoor meals, and relaxation. Such activities strengthen family bonds and instill a sense of responsibility for the shared environment, broadening the scope of kindness to include the natural world.

In contemplating renovations or remodeling efforts aimed at fostering kindness, it becomes evident that our homes' physical layout and design can significantly influence our interactions and relationships. From minor adjustments that enhance the functionality and warmth of a room to more extensive renovations that transform the very structure of our living spaces, each decision can contribute to creating an environment where kindness, empathy, and cooperation flourish.

In essence, designing spaces for kindness is about more than aesthetics or convenience; it's about intentionally creating environments that promote positive interactions, encourage sharing and cooperation, and support the emotional well-being of all who inhabit them. Through thoughtful design and organization, our homes can become catalysts for kindness, reflecting and reinforcing the values we hold dear and shaping our daily lives in profound and lasting ways.

Illustrative Stories

In the quest to cultivate kindness within the home, families around the globe adopt diverse and creative approaches, each tailoring their environment and daily practices to reinforce the values of empathy, cooperation, and respect. The tapestry of these efforts paints a vivid picture of the universal desire to nurture kind-hearted individuals. Let's look at some illustrative stories of families who have woven kindness into the very fabric of their lives, showcasing the rich diversity of paths taken toward this common goal.

In the bustling suburbs of a large metropolitan area, the Rivera family embarked on a unique journey to integrate kindness into their everyday lives. With two children aged eight and twelve, Maria and Carlos Rivera transformed their modest home into a sanctuary of empathy and understanding. One of their most notable initiatives was the "Wall of Kindness," a large bulletin board in the living room adorned with notes, drawings, and photographs capturing acts of kindness both received and given. This living collage not only served as a constant visual reminder of their family values but also as a conversation starter, encouraging family members and guests alike to share their experiences and reflections on kindness. Over time, the Wall of Kindness became a testament to the Rivera family's commitment, inspiring their children, friends, and neighbors to seek out and acknowledge kindness in their lives actively.

Halfway around the world, in a small village in the countryside, the Ng family demonstrates how kindness can flourish even in the most communal settings. With three generations living under one roof, the Ng family faced the challenge of balancing individual needs with collective harmony. Their solution was the creation of a "Kindness Garden," a communal space where each family member, from the youngest to the eldest, could contribute according to their ability. Whether planting vegetables, watering flowers, or simply enjoying the garden's beauty, each act contributed to a shared sense of purpose and well-being. The Kindness Garden became a symbol of the family's interdependence and mutual respect, illustrating how the acts of caring for nature and each other are intertwined.

In another corner of the world, the Johansson family in a Scandinavian city turned to technology to foster kindness among their teenage children. Recognizing the challenges of engaging teenagers in family activities, Anna and Erik Johansson developed a family app that allowed members to post daily acts of kindness, challenges, and words of encouragement. This digital platform facilitated communication among family members and enabled them to track their collective progress in building a kinder family culture. The app's success led to the introduction of "Kindness Missions," where the family volunteered at local shelters, participated in community clean-up events, and engaged in acts of kindness toward their neighbors, documenting their journey through the app. The Johansson family's innovative approach highlights the potential of technology to support and amplify efforts to cultivate kindness in the digital age.

The Thompson family in a quiet suburb found inspiration in literature to instill values of empathy and kindness in their children. Every week, the family dedicated an evening to "Kindness Storytime," where they read books emphasizing compassion, understanding, and respect for differences. These stories, ranging from classic tales to contemporary narratives, served as springboards for discussions about moral choices, the importance of empathy, and the impact of kindness on others. The Thompsons extended this practice beyond their family by organizing a monthly book swap in their community, encouraging other families to explore and share stories that celebrate kindness. This initiative enriched their own family's experience and fostered a sense of community and shared values among their neighbors.

Though distinct in their backgrounds and approaches, each of these families shares a joint commitment to creating environments that nurture kindness. Whether through visual reminders, communal projects, digital engagement, or the power of storytelling, their efforts demonstrate the myriad ways families can encourage empathy, cooperation, and respect. These stories serve as both inspiration and testament to the idea that kindness, in its many forms, is a universal language that transcends cultural, geographical, and generational boundaries.

Practical Tips

Creating a kindness-focused environment is an ongoing journey, and here are some practical tips to get started:

1. **Evaluate Your Space**: Look at your home with fresh eyes to identify areas that could be more conducive to sharing, cooperation, and kindness. Simple changes, like rearranging furniture to create cozy conversation spots, can make a big difference.

2. **Involve the Family**: Include family members in discussions about how to make your home a kinder place. This can be as simple as choosing a charity to support together or deciding on a family project that contributes to the community.

3. **Celebrate Kindness**: Create a visible space in your home, like a kindness bulletin board, where family members can post notes about acts of kindness they've witnessed or done. This not only celebrates kindness but also encourages more of it.

4. **Mindful Purchases**: Consider the impact of new purchases on the family dynamic. Opt for items encouraging collaboration or learning about other cultures, fostering empathy and understanding.

5. **Create Traditions**: Establish family traditions that revolve around acts of kindness, such as a monthly day of service or crafting homemade gifts for those in need. These traditions reinforce the value of kindness in a tangible, memorable way.

Reflective Conclusion

As we close this chapter on creating a kindness-focused environment, it's time for reflection. Assess your current living space and daily routines through the lens of kindness. Consider the physical layout of your home, the activities you prioritize as a family, and the ways you interact with one another. Are there areas where changes, even small ones, could foster a more supportive and compassionate atmosphere?

Challenging ourselves to make these changes is not always easy, but the rewards are immeasurable. A home that breathes kindness becomes a sanctuary for our family and all who enter. It becomes a place where the values of empathy, cooperation, and gratitude are not just spoken of but lived out daily.

Embrace this challenge with an open heart and a willingness to experiment. Remember, creating a kindness-focused environment is a journey, not a destination. Each step, no matter how small, is a step toward a more loving and compassionate world, beginning within the walls of our own homes.

Chapter 3:
Fostering Kindness Through Communication

Kind words can be short and easy to speak, but their echoes are truly endless. –Mother Teresa

Words kill, words give life; they're either poison or fruit—you choose. –Proverbs 18:21 (The Message)

The language of friendship is not words but meanings.
–Henry David Thoreau

A young boy named Liam and his mother, Emily, lived in the quiet town of Maplewood, nestled between rolling hills and whispering pines. Their home, a cozy cottage with a red door, was filled with the warm glow of laughter and the sweet scent of baking on the weekends. A single mother, Emily devoted her life to raising Liam with love and kindness, aware that her words and actions were the mirrors in which Liam saw his own worth.

One chilly autumn evening, as the sun dipped below the horizon, casting long shadows across the garden, Liam sat at the kitchen table, pencil in hand, brows furrowed over his homework. The room was quiet except for the soft ticking of the clock and the occasional rustle of paper. Emily watched her son from across the room, noticing the frustration etching deeper into his features.

Breaking the silence, she asked, "What's wrong, Liam?"

"I can't do this," Liam muttered, pushing the worksheet away. "It's too hard."

Emily approached, pulling up a chair beside him. "Let's take a look at it together," she suggested gently, her voice a soothing balm to Liam's growing distress.

As they worked through the problems, Emily's patience and encouragement slowly unraveled Liam's frustration. Each word she spoke was infused with belief in his abilities, starkly contrasting the self-doubt that had clouded his mind. "You're doing great, Liam. Look how far you've come already," she would say, "I know it's challenging, but I believe in you. You're capable of amazing things."

This was not the first time Emily had wielded the power of her words to uplift her son. From the earliest days of his childhood, she had been mindful of the language she used, understanding that her words carried the weight to either build up or tear down. She chose to build, to fortify, to inspire.

However, not all the children in Maplewood were as fortunate as Liam. Across the street lived another boy, Ethan, whose circumstances painted a starkly different picture. Ethan's parents, though not unloving, were often stressed and preoccupied, their words sometimes slipping into the realm of criticism and impatience.

"Why can't you get anything right?" they might say in moments of frustration or, "You're just not trying hard enough."

Though perhaps spoken in fleeting moments of exasperation, these words lingered in Ethan's mind, bringing doubt and fear that shadowed his perception of himself. Unlike Liam, who bloomed under the nurturing light of positive affirmation, Ethan wilted, his self-esteem and confidence eroding under the weight of words that tore down rather than built up.

The difference in the boys' self-images and attitudes toward challenges was palpable. Where Liam approached difficulties with resilience and a willingness to try, Ethan recoiled, haunted by the fear of not being "good enough."

The story of Liam and Ethan serves as a poignant reminder of the profound impact a parent's or caregiver's words can have on a child's development. In Liam's case, Emily's conscious choice to use her words as tools of empowerment and encouragement laid a foundation for kindness, self-confidence, and perseverance. For Ethan, the critical and discouraging words from his parents created barriers to self-esteem and kindness, both toward himself and others.

This tale underscores the vital importance of communication in nurturing kindness and compassion. The words we choose to use, especially in the role of a parent or caregiver, are powerful instruments that can shape a child's worldview, influence their interactions, and determine the path of their personal growth. As such, fostering kindness through communication is not merely about teaching children to be kind to others but about embodying the essence of kindness in every word we speak to them, setting the stage for a lifetime of empathy, understanding, and compassion.

Open and Honest Conversations About Kindness

In the mosaic of family life, where each day brings challenges and triumphs, the conversations we weave into the fabric of our daily interactions hold profound power. Among these, discussions about kindness are pivotal threads, essential for nurturing a culture of empathy, understanding, and genuine compassion within our families. Making conversations about kindness a regular facet of family life teaches children the importance of this virtue. It equips them with the heart to navigate the world with grace and empathy.

The Foundation of Kindness in Conversation

At the heart of fostering an environment where kindness flourishes is the commitment to open and honest conversations about what it means to be kind, the impact of our actions on others, and the significance of empathy in our interactions. These discussions are invaluable, for they offer more than just lessons; they provide a safe space for children to explore the complexities of human emotions and relationships, developing a deep-seated understanding of kindness that transcends mere actions.

Initiating Conversations About Kindness

Starting conversations about kindness need not be a daunting task. Often, the most profound discussions spring from the simplest moments or activities. Here are some practical tips for weaving these crucial conversations into the rhythm of everyday life:

Through Stories and Media

Books and movies with themes of kindness, empathy, and compassion serve as powerful conversation starters. After sharing a story or watching a film, discuss the characters' actions, the outcomes of these actions, and how they reflect the principles of kindness. Questions like, "How do you think the character felt when...?" or "What would you have done in that situation?" encourage children to put themselves in others' shoes, fostering empathy and deeper understanding.

Reflecting on Daily Interactions

Everyday interactions within the family and with others provide rich fodder for conversations about kindness. Reflecting on these interactions can be enlightening, offering insights into how our actions and words affect those around us. Discuss both positive experiences of kindness and instances where kindness was lacking, exploring the feelings and outcomes associated with these moments. This reflection not only highlights the value of kindness but also encourages mindfulness in future interactions.

Sharing Personal Experiences

Encourage family members to share their experiences of giving, receiving, or witnessing kindness. These personal stories make the concept of kindness tangible and relatable, showcasing its impact in real-life contexts. Sharing experiences of unkindness is equally essential, as it opens up discussions about responding to such situations with grace and understanding.

The Value of Honesty and Openness

Central to these conversations is the principle of honesty and openness. It is crucial to create a family culture where children feel safe to express their feelings and share their experiences without fear of judgment or dismissal. This openness fosters trust and strengthens the family bond, laying the groundwork for a supportive environment where kindness can thrive.

Encouraging Empathy and Understanding

As conversations about kindness unfold, emphasize the importance of empathy—putting oneself in another's shoes. Encourage children to consider the perspectives and feelings of others in various situations, fostering a deep-seated understanding of empathy as the foundation of kindness. These discussions should also extend to acknowledging and respecting differences and teaching children to embrace diversity with an open heart and mind.

Navigating Challenges with Kindness

Discuss how to navigate challenges and conflicts with kindness, focusing on the power of kind words and actions to diffuse tension and resolve disputes. Highlight the importance of forgiveness and understanding in overcoming misunderstandings and strengthening relationships. (More on this in a moment.)

Practical Applications of Kindness

Beyond discussions, encourage practical applications of kindness in daily life. This includes acts of service within the community, random acts of kindness for friends or neighbors, or ways to be kinder within the family. These actions, coupled with reflective discussions, reinforce the values of kindness in tangible ways.

Teaching Conflict Resolution Skills

Conflict is inevitable in the intricate dance of family life, where differing needs, personalities, and perspectives converge. Yet, within these moments of discord lies a golden opportunity to teach our children invaluable lessons in empathy, respect, and understanding. Conflict resolution skills are among the most crucial tools we can provide our children, equipping them to navigate disagreements with grace and emerge with relationships not only intact but strengthened. This section delves into practical strategies for teaching effective conflict resolution, emphasizing kindness and constructive outcomes.

The Foundation of Empathy and Respect

At the heart of resolving conflicts lies the ability to understand and respect the other person's perspective. This doesn't necessarily mean agreeing with their viewpoint but recognizing it as valid and worthy of consideration. Teaching children to approach conflicts with empathy—putting themselves in the other person's shoes—encourages a deeper understanding of the emotions and motivations at play.

Using "I" Statements

One of the most effective tools in the conflict resolution toolkit is using "I" statements. This communication strategy involves expressing one's feelings and needs without blaming or accusing the other person. For example, instead of saying, "You always take my things without asking," one might say, "I feel upset when my things are taken without permission because I value my privacy." This approach allows for expressing personal feelings and needs while minimizing defensiveness in the other person.

Finding Compromise

The goal of conflict resolution is not to "win" but to find a compromise that respects everyone's needs and feelings. This often involves creative problem-solving and negotiation, encouraging children to think beyond their immediate desires to achieve an acceptable solution for all parties involved.

Steps for Resolving Disagreements

To navigate conflicts effectively, it is helpful to follow a structured approach:

1. **Calm Down**: Teach children the importance of taking a moment to calm down before addressing a conflict. Deep breathing, counting to ten, or taking a short walk can help diffuse immediate emotions, making it easier to engage in constructive conversation.

2. **Express Feelings Using "I" Statements**: Encourage children to express their feelings using "I" statements, focusing on their emotions rather than assigning blame.

3. **Listen to the Other Person's Perspective**: Emphasize the importance of actively listening to the other person, showing genuine interest in understanding their feelings and viewpoints.

4. **Find a Compromise**: Work together to find a solution that meets the needs of both parties, emphasizing that compromise does not mean giving in but finding a middle ground.

5. **Apologize and Forgive**: Teach children the value of apologizing for any hurt caused and the power of forgiveness in moving forward.

Age-Appropriate Conflict Scenarios

Scenario 1: Sharing Toys (Ages 4-7)

Conflict: Two siblings argue over who gets to play with a favorite toy.

Resolution Strategy: Encourage them to express their feelings using "I" statements, such as "I feel sad when I don't get a turn with the toy." Guide them in brainstorming solutions, such as setting a timer for equal playtimes or choosing another game they can play together. This teaches them to negotiate and share, reinforcing that kindness and fairness are paramount.

Scenario 2: Group Projects (Ages 8-12)

Conflict: Disagreement in a school group project about who does what part.

Resolution Strategy: Teach the children to discuss their strengths and interests, using "I" statements to express their preferences and concerns. Encourage them to listen to each other's perspectives and find a division of labor that matches each member's strengths. This demonstrates that empathy and respect can lead to better teamwork and outcomes.

Scenario 3: Social Media Misunderstandings (Ages 13-18)

Conflict: A misunderstanding arises from an online comment among friends, leading to hurt feelings.

Resolution Strategy: Advise the teen to address the issue directly with the friend involved, expressing their feelings with "I" statements and asking for the friend's perspective. Highlight the importance of discussing sensitive matters in person or over the phone rather than through text, where misinterpretations are common and often exacerbate the issue. This teaches the value of clear, empathetic communication in resolving misunderstandings.

Reinforcing Kindness in Conflict Resolution

The overarching message should always come back to kindness in teaching conflict resolution skills. Emphasizing that every conflict is an opportunity to practice empathy, respect, and understanding reinforces the idea that kindness is not just an act but a way of navigating the world. By guiding children through age-appropriate conflict scenarios with this mindset, we not only equip them with the skills to resolve disagreements constructively but also instill the values of compassion and kindness that will serve them throughout their lives.

The art of conflict resolution, rooted in empathy and respect, is among the most precious lessons we can impart to our children. It prepares them to face inevitable disagreements and emerge from these challenges with more robust, compassionate relationships. Through open communication, honest expression of feelings, and a commitment to understanding and compromise, we can teach our children that conflicts, handled with kindness, can lead to growth, deeper connections, and a more empathetic world.

Emphasizing Tone and Delivery in Communication

In the intricate dance of human interaction, the subtleties of how we communicate—our tone of voice, body language, and choice of words—play a pivotal role in shaping the perceptions and feelings of those around us. It's a timeless truth, often encapsulated in the phrase, "It's not just what we say, but how we say it," that underscores the profound impact of our communication style. This understanding is especially crucial when teaching children about kindness and empathy, as it equips them with the skills for more effective and positive interactions. This section explores the nuances of tone and delivery in communication, offering strategies and exercises to help parents guide their children in understanding and mastering these aspects.

The Power of Tone

The tone of voice, often more eloquent than words, carries the emotional weight of our messages. A kind word spoken with a harsh tone can easily be perceived as criticism, while constructive feedback, delivered with warmth and care, is more likely to be received positively. With their keen sensitivity to emotional cues, children are especially attuned to the tone of voice, which can significantly influence their understanding and emotional response.

Teaching the Impact of Tone

Parents can teach children about the impact of tone through simple exercises and games. One effective method is role-playing, where parent and child switch roles in a scripted scenario, each delivering the same line with different tones—angry, happy, sad, sarcastic—and observing how the message's perception changes with the tone. This exercise makes learning about tone engaging and interactive and enhances children's empathy by encouraging them to consider how their words might affect others.

The Significance of Body Language

Body language, the silent symphony of human communication, speaks volumes without uttering a word. A welcoming smile, open posture, or a gentle nod can convey interest, openness, and warmth, reinforcing the kindness of our words. Conversely, crossed arms, avoidance of eye contact, or a dismissive gesture can create barriers to communication, regardless of the words spoken.

Exploring Body Language with Children

Parents can explore the importance of body language with their children through observation and mimicry games. Watching scenes from children's shows or movies on mute and guessing the characters' feelings based on their body language can be an insightful and enjoyable way to highlight non-verbal communication's impact. Practicing mirroring each other's body language in various emotional states further reinforces understanding and empathy.

Choosing Words Wisely

The words we choose are the bridge between thought and understanding, carrying our intentions across the chasm of individual perspective. Teaching children to select kind, clear, and considerate words can significantly affect how their messages are received. Emphasizing the importance of thoughtful word choice encourages children to communicate with kindness and respect, fostering positive interactions.

Exercises in Word Choice

A valuable exercise in exploring word choice involves presenting children with different scenarios and asking them to respond using different sets of words—first with neutral or vague language, then with words carefully chosen for kindness and clarity. Discussing the different reactions each set of words might elicit can illuminate the power of word choice in communication.

Modeling Positive Communication Habits

I know I'm going to sound like a broken record on this, but the most powerful tool in teaching children about tone, body language, and word choice is modeling these behaviors ourselves. When parents communicate with kindness, respect, and empathy, they provide a living example for their children to emulate. This means being mindful of our tone, even in frustration, being aware of our body language, ensuring it matches our words, and choosing words that convey our messages clearly and kindly.

Demonstrating Kindness in Communication

Modeling positive communication also involves demonstrating how to navigate misunderstandings and conflicts with kindness. Showing children how to apologize, clarify misconceptions, and express feelings without blame or judgment teaches them that kindness in communication is not just about preventing negative interactions but also about repairing them.

Illustrative Stories

The power of effective communication to foster kindness and understanding is profound and transformative in human interactions. The following stories illuminate this truth, offering real-life examples of how empathy, clarity, and intentionality in communication can lead to positive outcomes, weaving lessons of kindness into the fabric of everyday life.

The Apology that Mended Fences

In a small-town community, two neighbors, Sarah and Jenna, found themselves at odds over a boundary dispute. A minor disagreement escalated into a situation where harsh words were exchanged, and a once-friendly relationship turned sour. The conflict reached a point where both parties avoided each other, letting the disagreement cast a shadow over their lives.

One crisp autumn evening, Sarah stepped back, reflecting on the situation. She realized the ongoing tension was not worth the emotional cost and decided to extend an olive branch. She wrote Jenna a heartfelt letter, expressing her regret for the harsh words and the role she played in escalating the conflict. She emphasized her desire to resolve the disagreement amicably, valuing their relationship over being right.

Jenna, touched by Sarah's sincerity and willingness to apologize, responded with her own letter, reciprocating the sentiments of regret and a desire to move forward positively. This exchange led to a face-to-face conversation where both expressed their feelings and perspectives openly and respectfully. Through effective communication and a mutual willingness to listen, they found a compromise that respected their needs, mending the literal and metaphorical fence between them.

The Lesson in Listening

Mark, a high school teacher, noticed that one of his students, Alex, had become withdrawn and disengaged in class, a stark contrast to the enthusiastic participant he once was. Concerned, Mark decided to reach out and invite Alex for a chat after school.

During their conversation, Mark practiced active listening, giving Alex his full attention and encouraging him to share his feelings without interruption or judgment. As Alex opened up, he revealed struggles with self-esteem and feeling overwhelmed by academic pressures. Mark listened empathetically, acknowledging Alex's feelings and sharing his experiences with overcoming challenges.

This conversation marked a turning point for Alex. Knowing he had a supportive adult who understood and cared about his well-being made a significant difference. Mark continued to check in with Alex, offering guidance and support, which helped Alex regain his confidence and re-engage with his studies. This story highlights the transformative power of listening—an act of kindness that can provide comfort, understanding, and a path forward during challenging times.

The Bridge of Words

In a bustling city, a community center faced closure due to funding cuts, much to the dismay of the neighborhood that relied on its services. Emma, a long-time volunteer at the center, was determined to save it. She organized a meeting with city officials and prepared a presentation that not only highlighted the center's value to the community but also addressed potential concerns and solutions regarding funding.

Emma's presentation was a masterclass in effective communication. She spoke with clarity, passion, and respect, weaving in stories from community members whose lives were positively impacted by the center. Her tone was one of collaboration, not confrontation, inviting the officials to be part of a solution that would benefit the entire community.

Moved by Emma's presentation and the community's outpouring of support, the city officials agreed to work together to find the necessary funding to keep the center open. Emma's ability to communicate kindly and effectively—choosing her words carefully, delivering her message with empathy, and focusing on mutual benefits—led to a kind and beneficial outcome that preserved a vital community resource.

Lessons Learned

These stories, unique in their context and characters, share a common thread—the transformative power of kind communication in leading to practical outcomes. The lessons they offer are universal:

- **The Power of Apology**: A sincere apology can bridge the widest gaps, turning conflict into compromise and restoring harmony.

- **The Importance of Listening**: Sometimes, the kindest thing we can do is listen—truly listen—to understand the feelings and needs of others.

- **The Strength in Collaboration**: Approaching conversations intending to collaborate rather than confront can lead to solutions that benefit everyone involved.

These examples show that effective communication, rooted in empathy, clarity, and kindness, can change outcomes, mend relationships, and strengthen communities. These stories inspire and remind us of the profound impact our words and actions can have on the world around us.

Practical Tips

Improving kind communication within the family is an ongoing journey tailored to adapt to the evolving dynamics of family life. Below are concrete strategies designed to foster an environment where empathy, understanding, and kindness are at the forefront of every interaction. These tips are segmented to address various ages, situations, and stages of family life, ensuring that every family member can contribute to and benefit from a culture of kind communication.

For Young Children (Ages 3-7)

1. **Model Kind Communication**: Children in this age group learn by observing. Use polite words like "please" and "thank you" consistently, address others respectfully, and show patience in your interactions. Demonstrate active listening by giving your full attention (put the phone down!) when your child speaks, affirming their feelings and thoughts.

2. **Use Stories and Role-play**: Incorporate books and stories with themes of kindness and empathy into your reading time. Afterward, engage in role-play based on these stories, allowing your child to practice expressing kindness and understanding through play.

3. **Emotion Identification Games**: Play games that help children identify and name their feelings. Use drawings, flashcards, or facial expressions to guess the emotion. This builds emotional intelligence, a key component of kind communication.

For School-Aged Children (Ages 8-12)

1. **Family Communication Meetings**: Hold regular family meetings where members can share their thoughts, feelings, and experiences from the week. Encourage open and respectful dialogue, teaching children to express themselves clearly and listen to others empathetically.

2. **Conflict Resolution Skills**: Introduce basic conflict resolution skills. Teach them to use "I" statements to express their feelings without blaming others and brainstorm solutions to disagreements that respect everyone's needs.

3. **Kindness Challenges**: Implement weekly kindness challenges where each family member aims to perform specific acts of kindness. Discuss these actions and their impacts during family meals, reinforcing the value of kind communication through deeds as well as words.

For Teenagers (Ages 13-18)

1. **Digital Communication Etiquette**: Discuss the importance of kindness in digital communication. Explore the impact of tone and language in texts and social media, emphasizing the difference between online and face-to-face

interactions and the potential for misinterpretation.

2. **Active Listening Practice**: Engage in exercises that enhance active listening skills, such as repeating back what the other person said before responding, to ensure understanding and validation of the speaker's perspective.

3. **Empathy Building Activities**: Encourage teenagers to volunteer or participate in community service projects. Reflect on these experiences together, discussing the insights gained about different life situations and the importance of empathy and kindness in all interactions.

For Parents and Caregivers

1. **Self-Reflection and Adjustment**: Regularly reflect on your communication style and its impact on your family. Be open to feedback and willing to adjust your behavior to model kindness more effectively.

2. **Stress Management**: Recognize how stress affects communication and implement stress-reduction techniques like mindfulness, exercise, or hobbies. Sharing these practices with your

family can improve overall communication and reduce instances of conflict.

3. **Seek Understanding First**: In moments of disagreement or tension, prioritize understanding the other person's perspective before responding. This approach fosters a more empathetic and kind communication environment.

Across All Stages of Family Life

1. **Use Visual Reminders**: Post quotes, images, or lists around the home that remind family members of the importance of kind communication. These can serve as prompts to practice kindness even in challenging moments.

2. **Celebrate Kind Communication**: Acknowledge and celebrate instances of kind communication within the family. Reinforcing these behaviors encourages their continuation, whether through verbal praise, a note of appreciation, or a family reward.

3. **Create a Family Communication Charter**: Collaborate to create a set of communication guidelines that reflect your family's values and commitment to kindness. Review and update

this charter periodically to adapt to your family's evolving needs and circumstances.

Families can cultivate an environment where kind communication thrives by integrating these practical tips into daily family life. Through intentional practice, empathy, and understanding, every family member can contribute to a culture of kindness that extends beyond the home into every interaction.

Reflective Conclusion

As we draw Chapter 3 to a close, I invite you to pause and reflect on how communication is shared within your family. The essence of kind communication—rooted in empathy, understanding, and respect—forms the cornerstone of healthy, nurturing relationships within our households and beyond.

Consider the following questions to further your growth in kindness through communication:

1. **How often do I actively listen to my family members?** When others speak, reflect on the quality of your attention. Are you fully present, or are thoughts and distractions pulling you away? Active listening is a gift of presence, a fundamental act of kindness that acknowledges the speaker's value and dignity.

2. **Do my tone, body language, and words align with my intentions?** Think about recent interactions. Were your non-verbal cues in harmony with your words, reinforcing your message? Or did they send mixed signals, diluting or contradicting what you sought to convey? The unity of our expressions, gestures, and language powerfully impacts the clarity and kindness of our communication.

3. **In moments of conflict, how do I contribute to resolution and understanding?** Consider your role in resolving disagreements. Do you approach conflicts to understand and find common ground, or do positions and the need to be right take precedence? Reflecting on this can illuminate pathways to more empathetic and constructive conflict resolution.

4. **What steps can I take to model kind communication for my children?** Children learn how to interact with the world primarily from their parents. Think about the communication patterns you're modeling. Are they the ones you wish your children to emulate? Identifying ways to demonstrate kind communication can set powerful examples for your children.

As we set goals for fostering kindness through improved dialogue within our families, we must approach this process with grace and patience—both for ourselves and our family members. Growth and change in communication habits take time, intention, and practice. By committing to this journey, we open the door to deeper connections, enriched by the mutual respect, empathy, and love that kind communication nurtures.

Chapter 4:
Nurturing Empathy and Compassion in Children

Empathy is about finding echoes of another person in yourself.
—Mohsin Hamid

The great gift of human beings is that we have the power of empathy. —Meryl Streep

You never really understand a person until you consider things from his point of view... Until you climb inside of his skin and walk around in it. —Harper Lee, To Kill a Mockingbird

In the warm embrace of a friend's home, where laughter danced through the air and the joy of new life mingled with the hum of conversation, I witnessed a moment of pure, unscripted empathy that would forever change my perspective on nurturing compassion in children. The occasion was a celebration of new beginnings, marking the arrival of our friends' third child, a gathering vibrant with the energy of life and the promise of future memories. Amidst the festivities, a scene unfolded that captured the essence of empathy in its most genuine form.

My son, Caleb, at the time, our only child, full of spirited energy and curiosity, was among several children playing in the living room. With eyes that sparkled with the innocent wonder of youth, Caleb had an infectious joy, drawing the eye and warming the heart.

The youngest member of the gathering, two-week-old Abby, found herself momentarily distraught, having accidentally cast her comfort blanket beyond the confines of her infant recliner chair. Her sudden and sharp tears pierced the atmosphere, a stark contrast to the prevailing mirth. Without hesitation, Caleb ceased his play, his young mind recognizing distress in another soul. He navigated the sea of toys and legs with purpose and kindness, reaching Abby's side with the determination of one bound by an invisible thread of understanding.

With the gentle care of a seasoned caregiver, Caleb retrieved the blanket, carefully arranging it around Abby, and offered a hug—a gesture of warmth and reassurance that spoke volumes of his innate capacity for empathy. Abby's tears subsided, soothed by the simple act of kindness from one so young. Caleb, his mission of compassion complete, returned to his play.

This moment, witnessed from the sanctuary of the couch, coffee in my hand, catalyzed a conversation between my wife and me about our commitment to fostering this essential aspect of kindness in our children.

As I've reflected on this incident over the years, it has illuminated the foundational elements of emotional intelligence: the ability to recognize emotions in others, to respond with appropriate actions, and to connect on a level that transcends words. Caleb's actions were not the result of explicit instruction but an automatic response born of his inherent empathy. This served as a potent realization that children are keen observers of emotions and capable of extraordinary sensitivity to the feelings of those around them.

To cultivate such empathy and compassion in children, we must recognize and celebrate these moments of intuitive kindness, using them as opportunities to reinforce the values of understanding and care. Through consistent practice and reflection, guided by the examples set by parents and caregivers, children learn to navigate the complexities of human emotions with grace and empathy. This story of Caleb and Abby, a simple yet profound interaction, stands as a testament to the potential within each child to develop a deep, abiding capacity for empathy and compassion, shaping their character and interactions with the world around them.

Teaching Children to Recognize and Understand Emotions

Understanding and managing one's emotions and recognizing and responding to the feelings of others are critical skills for healthy development. This section explores the concept of emotional literacy, which is the ability to identify, understand, and respond to emotions in oneself and others. Emotional literacy lays the groundwork for developing empathy by recognizing and appreciating how others feel.

The Importance of Emotional Literacy

Emotional literacy is not just an educational tool; it's a life skill that influences our interactions, decision-making, and relationships. Emotional literacy helps children navigate social complexities, fosters healthy relationships, and supports emotional and mental health.

Studies have shown that children taught to identify and manage their emotions from a young age tend to have better social outcomes, including reduced instances of bullying, higher academic achievements, and stronger friendships (Schokman et al., 2014; Malik & Shujja, 2013; Paavola, 2017).

Strategies for Teaching Emotional Literacy

Teaching children to recognize and understand emotions can be integrated into daily life through various engaging and age-appropriate methods:

1. **Emotion Cards**: Use cards with different facial expressions or scenarios depicting various emotions. Encourage children to name the emotion and discuss a time they felt that way, enhancing their ability to identify and relate to different feelings.

2. **Storytelling and Role-playing**: Incorporate stories that highlight a range of emotions. After reading, engage children in role-playing exercises

based on the story's characters, allowing them to explore the emotions experienced by the characters in different situations.

3. **Reflective Listening**: Practice reflective listening by repeating back to your child, in your own words, what they've said about how they feel. This validates their feelings and helps them understand their emotions more intensely.

4. **Emotion Diary**: Older children can benefit from keeping an emotion diary. They can note their feelings throughout the day and reflect on what triggered them. This encourages self-awareness and helps children recognize patterns in their emotional responses. (There's an app for that. Day One (iOS and Android) is a simple journaling tool. More in-depth options are plentiful, too.)

The Role of Parents in Emotional Education

Parents play a pivotal role in their children's emotional education. By validating their children's feelings and modeling healthy emotional expression, parents set the foundation for emotional literacy.

1. **Validating Feelings**: Acknowledge and validate your child's emotions, even if they seem trivial or challenging to understand. This validation

communicates that all feelings are acceptable and that you are safe to share with.

2. **Modeling Emotional Expression**: Remember Chapter 1? Children learn to express emotions primarily by observing their parents. Model healthy ways of expressing feelings, including talking about your emotions, using "I feel" statements, and demonstrating constructive ways to manage strong emotions.

3. **Encouraging Open Communication**: Foster an environment where emotions can be openly discussed without judgment. Regular family meetings or check-ins can be an effective forum for sharing feelings and discussing emotional challenges.

4. **Setting Boundaries**: Teach children that while all emotions are valid, there are appropriate and inappropriate ways to express them. Setting clear boundaries and consequences for actions helps children learn to manage their feelings responsibly.

Developing emotional literacy is a lifelong journey that begins in childhood. By equipping children with the tools to understand and express their emotions, parents lay the groundwork for empathy, resilience, and emotional well-being. This foundation enhances personal relationships and academic success and prepares children to navigate the world's complexities with kindness, understanding, and emotional intelligence.

Encouraging Perspective and Empathy

In the rich tapestry of human experience, empathy—the ability to understand and share another person's feelings—is a profound force for connection and understanding. Too many folks either confuse or equate sympathy and empathy, but there's a big difference between the two concepts; sympathy is feeling *for* someone, whereas empathy is feeling *with* someone. It's through empathy that we transcend our own perspectives to truly appreciate and enter into the emotions and viewpoints of others. Developing this capacity is crucial for children's emotional intelligence, nurturing compassionate relationships, and fostering a sense of global citizenship. Here are some various activities and practices parents and caregivers can employ to encourage children to consider others' perspectives and cultivate empathy.

Role-playing Games

One of the most effective tools for teaching perspective-taking and empathy is role-playing. This interactive activity allows children to step into someone else's shoes, if only for a moment, to experience a situation from a different viewpoint. Parents can create scenarios that mirror a child's real-life situations—disagreements with a friend, feeling left out, or witnessing someone else being teased. Through role-playing, children can explore not just their own feelings and reactions but also those of the other individuals involved.

A role-playing game might involve taking turns playing different roles in a scenario, such as a new student at school or someone who has lost a pet. After acting out the scenario, discuss as a family what emotions each character might have felt and why. This discussion deepens the learning experience, reinforcing the connection between actions, perspectives, and emotions.

Discussing Characters' Feelings in Stories

Stories, whether told through books, movies, or even video games, offer a window into characters' emotional lives that children might not encounter in their everyday lives. After sharing a story, take the opportunity to discuss the characters' feelings and motivations. Ask questions like, "Why do you think the character felt that way?" or "How would you feel if you were in that situation?" These discussions can help children understand that their feelings and experiences are not universal, opening their minds to the diverse ways people react to and view the world.

Imagining Others' Perspectives

Encourage children to imagine how someone else might feel in a given situation as a regular part of your family's conversations. This could be as simple as observing a scene at the park and imagining the stories of the people you see or discussing the day's events and contemplating how different people involved might have felt and why. Regularly considering others' viewpoints helps children naturally start seeing the world from multiple perspectives, not just their own.

Emotion Guessing Games

Playing games that involve guessing others' emotions based on facial expressions, body language, or a described scenario can be fun and educational. Use pictures from magazines or scenes from family movies, or imagine scenarios together and guess what the person might feel. This activity not only improves children's ability to recognize emotions in others but also encourages them to think about what might cause someone to feel a certain way.

Frequent, Open Discussions About Emotions and Viewpoints

Integrating open discussions about emotions, viewpoints, and empathy into the fabric of family life lays the groundwork for a compassionate and understanding home environment. Regularly set aside time to share how everyone's day went, focusing not just on events but on the emotions and perspectives involved. Encourage children to share not only their own experiences but also their thoughts on how others might have felt during those experiences.

The Empathy Jar

Create an "empathy jar" in your home where family members can write down and deposit moments when they felt empathy, observed a kind act, or saw a situation from someone else's perspective. Regularly empty the jar and discuss its contents, celebrating these moments of empathy and perspective-taking. This tangible reminder of empathy's importance in your family's life reinforces its value and encourages everyone to keep looking for ways to understand and connect with others.

Encouraging Acts of Kindness Toward Others

In a world that often emphasizes individual success and competition, intentionally cultivating kindness is a beacon of hope, guiding us toward a more empathetic and compassionate society. Teaching our children to engage in acts of kindness not only enriches their own lives but also has a ripple effect, touching the lives of others in ways we might never fully comprehend. This section explores how families can integrate acts of kindness into their daily routines, turning every day into an opportunity to make the world a little brighter.

The Importance of Kindness in Daily Life

Kindness, in its essence, is the choice to extend love, consideration, and help to others without expecting anything in return. It's a fundamental human value that transcends cultural, religious, and societal differences. Encouraging children to practice kindness helps them develop empathy, strengthens their social bonds, and enhances their emotional well-being. By incorporating acts of kindness into daily routines, families can reinforce the message that kindness is not just an occasional gesture but a way of life.

Setting Kindness Goals

One practical approach to fostering habitual kindness is setting kindness goals. This might involve challenging each family member to perform a specific number of kind acts each week. The key is to make these goals attainable and specific, such as "help a classmate with a difficult task" or "write a thank-you note to someone who made a difference in your day." These goals encourage children to actively look for opportunities to be kind, making empathy and consideration a conscious part of their decision-making process.

Keeping a Kindness Journal

A kindness journal serves as a powerful tool for reflection, allowing children (and adults) to record their acts of kindness, the reactions they observed, and how the experience made them feel. Regularly reviewing this journal as a family can provide insights into the impact of kindness on both the giver and receiver, reinforcing the value of these actions and encouraging continued practice. This reflection process helps children see the tangible outcomes of their kindness, fostering a deeper understanding of empathy and compassion.

Incorporating Kindness into Daily Routines

Integrating acts of kindness into daily routines can be both spontaneous and planned. Here are examples of how families can encourage kindness in everyday life:

1. **Compliment Someone**: Teach children the power of a sincere compliment and encourage them to compliment friends, teachers, or family members. A simple "I like your drawing" or "You did a great job in the game today" can significantly impact someone's day.

2. **Volunteer Together**: Choose a cause or organization to support as a family. Whether participating in a local clean-up, serving meals at a shelter, or spending time with older adults,

volunteering together benefits the community and strengthens family bonds.

3. **Random Acts of Kindness**: Encourage children to engage in random acts of kindness, such as leaving a kind note for a neighbor, paying for the person behind them in line at a café, or offering to help carry groceries. These spontaneous gestures of kindness highlight the joy of giving without expectation.

4. **Kindness in Nature**: Promote kindness toward the environment by engaging in activities like planting trees, picking up litter during walks, or setting up a bird feeder in the backyard. These actions teach children to extend their empathy toward the planet and all its inhabitants.

Examples of Simple Acts of Kindness

- **Writing thank-you notes**: Encourage children to write thank-you notes for teachers, coaches, or family members, expressing gratitude for their support and care.

- **Sharing with others**: Teach children the value of sharing, whether sharing their snack with a friend who forgot theirs or donating toys they no longer use.

- **Being a friend**: Encourage children to befriend someone new at school, invite someone who is alone to play, or offer a listening ear to a friend in need.

The Collective Impact of Kindness

Every act of kindness, no matter how small, contributes to a more empathetic and compassionate world. By encouraging our children to engage in acts of kindness and reflecting on these experiences together, we nurture their emotional and social development and sow the seeds for a kinder, more understanding society. As families, we can make kindness a daily practice, transforming ordinary moments into extraordinary opportunities to connect, support, and uplift those around us. In doing so, we teach our children that they have the power to make a positive difference in the world, one act of kindness at a time.

Illustrative Stories

Let me offer three concise narratives that showcase children's development of empathy and compassion. Each story highlights their behavior's positive impact and empathy's ripple effect on their relationships and communities.

The Lemonade Stand for a Cause

Two children, Mia and Lucas, decided to set up a lemonade stand in the heart of a bustling suburb. Unlike typical ventures aiming for personal gain, they dedicated their effort to raising money for the local animal shelter. Having recently adopted a rescue dog, Mia felt a deep empathy for animals in need. Lucas, inspired by his friend's compassion, eagerly joined the cause.

Their lemonade stand, adorned with handmade signs and pictures of animals they hoped to help, quickly drew the community's attention. Their genuine concern and empathy were palpable as they shared the animals' stories with each customer. The children's initiative raised a significant sum for the shelter and inspired others in their neighborhood to think about how they could contribute to a cause greater than themselves.

The Birthday Gift of Giving

For her tenth birthday, instead of asking for gifts, Sophie requested her friends and family to bring donations to the local food bank. Sophie's decision came after a school trip to the food bank, where she learned about food insecurity and its impact on people in her city. This experience deeply moved her and sparked a desire to help.

Sophie's birthday party became a gathering with a purpose, as each guest arrived with bags of food to donate. The act of giving collectively not only made

Sophie's birthday memorable but also educated her friends about empathy and compassion toward those in need. The food collected during the party provided meals for several families, illustrating the significant impact of collective kindness.

Sophie's compassionate birthday choice left a lasting impression on her peers, encouraging them to think creatively about how they can make a difference in the lives of others.

The New Student Ambassador

When Aiden noticed the new student, Eli, struggling to fit in at school, he remembered how he felt when he was the new kid a year ago. With empathy driving his actions, Aiden approached Eli and offered to show him around, introducing him to other classmates and inviting him to join their lunch table.

Aiden's kindness toward Eli didn't go unnoticed. It set a precedent in the classroom, where inclusivity and kindness became the norm, not the exception. Aiden's initial act of empathy toward Eli encouraged others to extend the same warmth and welcome to all new students.

This narrative underscores the importance of empathy in fostering an inclusive and supportive community. Aiden's willingness to put himself in Eli's shoes and act on it had a transformative effect on their classroom environment, promoting a culture of kindness and acceptance.

Each of these stories, woven from the threads of empathy and compassion, showcases the profound impact that children, through their innate kindness and understanding, can have on their world. Whether it's raising awareness and funds for a cause, transforming personal celebrations into acts of giving, or fostering inclusivity and support among peers, these narratives illuminate the ripple effect of empathy. Through these acts of kindness, children develop deeper emotional intelligence and inspire those around them, proving that empathy is a powerful force for positive change.

Reflective Conclusion

As we draw this chapter to a close, I again invite you to pause and reflect on our kindness journey thus far. This chapter has woven together the fabric of understanding, showcasing the inherent value of empathy and compassion and the transformative impact these virtues can have on our children, our families, and the wider world. Through practical activities, illustrative stories, and strategic advice, we've explored how families can cultivate these essential qualities, laying the groundwork for a future marked by deeper connections and a more compassionate society.

As we consider the path forward, it's vital to engage in a personal assessment of how empathy and compassion are valued and demonstrated within our own families. Reflect on the following questions to guide this introspection:

1. **How often do we discuss feelings and emotions in our family?** Consider whether conversations about emotions are a regular occurrence. Do family members feel comfortable expressing their feelings openly and without judgment?

2. **In what ways have I modeled empathy and compassion to my children?** Reflect on your actions and words. Think about the moments you've demonstrated understanding and care, not just toward family members but also toward strangers, friends, and the community.

3. **How do we respond to conflicts and challenges within our family?** Evaluate whether conflicts are approached with a mindset geared toward understanding and resolution, prioritizing empathy even in disagreement.

4. **What opportunities for acts of kindness have we embraced as a family?** Consider both the planned and spontaneous acts of kindness in which your family has participated. Reflect on their impact on your family and those you've helped.

5. **How can we further integrate empathy and compassion into our daily lives?** Think about practical steps your family can take to deepen your practice of these virtues, from volunteering and community service to simple daily acts of kindness and understanding.

As you ponder these questions, remember that nurturing empathy and compassion is a continuous journey, one that evolves and deepens over time. It's a path marked by learning, growth, and the joy of seeing the world through the eyes of another. Again, friends, by valuing and demonstrating empathy and compassion within our families, we enrich our lives and contribute to a kinder, more understanding world.

Chapter 5:
Handling Challenges and Setbacks With Kindness

The true measure of a man is how he treats someone who can do him absolutely no good. –Samuel Johnson

When we give cheerfully and accept gratefully, everyone is blessed. –Maya Angelou

Courage doesn't always roar. Sometimes courage is the quiet voice at the end of the day saying, 'I will try again tomorrow.' –Mary Anne Radmacher

Facing life's challenges with kindness is not merely an act of grace; it's a profound strategy for resilience that can transform obstacles into opportunities for growth, connection, and positive change. Through the lens of kindness, setbacks become lessons in compassion, patience, and understanding, fostering an environment where individuals can thrive despite adversity. Let's explore three narratives that illuminate the transformative power of approaching life's difficulties with kindness.

The Community Garden

The local community garden had fallen into disrepair in a small town affected by an economic downturn. Vandalism and neglect had left the once-thriving plots barren, much to the residents' dismay. Amidst this despair, Elena, a retired teacher in the community, saw an opportunity not just for restoration but for reconnection.

Elena organized a community meeting, addressing the vandalism not with anger but with an invitation for understanding and collaboration. She proposed that the garden's revival could serve as a project for the town's youth, giving them a sense of purpose and responsibility. Elena's kindness and genuine concern for the young people, whom many had dismissed as troublemakers, transformed the narrative.

Under her guidance, the community came together, with teenagers taking the lead in repairing and replanting the garden. The project revitalized the space and mended broken ties within the community. Acts of vandalism ceased as the youths took pride in their contributions, and the garden flourished again, symbolizing resilience rooted in kindness.

The Bridge Between Rival Teams

A high school basketball game turned tense as rivalry spirit flared, leading to a heated exchange between players from opposing teams. The conflict reached a point where it threatened to overshadow the sport's spirit of sportsmanship and respect. That's when Coach Thompson intervened, not with disciplinary actions but with an invitation for dialogue.

He organized a joint team meeting, emphasizing kindness, empathy, and mutual respect. He encouraged players to share their backgrounds, challenges, and aspirations within and outside the sport. This act of kindness, creating a safe space for open communication, transformed rivalry into understanding and respect.

The teams left the meeting with a newfound appreciation for one another. The remainder of the season saw a significant decrease in conflicts, with players often seen supporting each other, regardless of team affiliation. Coach Thompson's kindness fostered a sense of community and sportsmanship that extended beyond the basketball court.

The Kindness Quilt

When Sarah, a fourth-grader, faced bullying at school, her mother, Lisa, sought a solution that would address the issue with compassion rather than confrontation. Lisa proposed a class project: a kindness quilt. Each student would contribute a square decorated with words or images representing kindness, which would be sewn together into a quilt for the classroom.

As Sarah and her classmates worked on their quilt squares, they discussed what kindness meant to them, sharing personal stories and listening to others. The project catalyzed change, creating an atmosphere of empathy and understanding within the class. Students who had once stood by or participated in the bullying began to see Sarah in a new light, and the bullying ceased.

The kindness quilt hung proudly in the classroom, a constant reminder of the power of empathy and the positive impact of approaching challenges with kindness.

It transformed the class dynamic, fostering an environment where all students felt valued and included.

These stories underscore the value of kindness as a tool for resilience and a powerful force for positive change. In the face of challenges and setbacks, kindness offers a path forward, one that embraces understanding, fosters connection, and cultivates a culture of compassion and resilience.

Teaching Resilience Through Kindness

Resilience, the ability to bounce back from setbacks, challenges, and failures, is a critical life skill, one that is nurtured not just through experiences of hardship but through the lens of kindness. This section explores how parents and caregivers can model resilience in their own lives and communicate these experiences to their children, emphasizing the role of self-kindness in overcoming life's inevitable obstacles. By integrating practical tips and strategies, we aim to equip families with the tools to foster a resilient spirit underpinned by compassion and self-care.

Modeling Resilience in Everyday Life

Children learn resilience by observing the adults around them. When parents face challenges, whether minor daily hassles or significant setbacks, they have a unique opportunity to model resilience in action. Discussing these experiences with children, emphasizing the problem-solving strategies employed and the emotional journey navigated, can offer invaluable lessons.

1. **Share Your Stories**: Be open about times you've faced difficulties and how you overcame them. Highlight the importance of perseverance, problem-solving, and seeking support when needed. These can be powerful teaching moments.

2. **Demonstrate Healthy Coping Strategies**: Let children see you practicing self-care and positive coping strategies, such as exercise, reading, or engaging in a hobby. Explain how these activities help manage stress and nurture resilience.

3. **Involve Children in Problem-Solving**: When facing family challenges, involve children in brainstorming solutions. This empowers them and teaches them that facing problems is a collaborative and constructive process.

The Importance of Self-Kindness

Self-kindness is a critical component of resilience. It involves treating oneself with compassion and understanding in the face of mistakes or failures rather than indulging in self-criticism. Encouraging children to practice self-kindness can significantly impact their ability to navigate setbacks positively.

1. **Teach Mindfulness Exercises**: Mindfulness can help children become more aware of their thoughts and feelings without judgment. Simple breathing exercises, guided meditations, or spending time in nature can foster a mindful approach to experiences.

2. **Encourage Positive Self-Talk**: Help children identify negative self-talk and replace it with positive affirmations. Phrases like "I can learn from this mistake" or "I am doing my best" can transform their inner dialogue, reinforcing resilience.

3. **Celebrate Effort, Not Just Outcome**: Emphasize the value of effort and learning in the face of challenges. Celebrating attempts and progress, rather than just successes, teaches children that resilience is about growth and perseverance.

Strategies for Encouraging Resilience Through Kindness

Fostering resilience through kindness involves a multifaceted approach, integrating practices that nurture self-compassion, empathy, and constructive problem-solving.

1. **Create a Kindness Ritual**: Establish family rituals that celebrate acts of kindness, both toward oneself and others. One such ritual could be a weekly sharing circle in which each family member highlights a kind act they've performed or received.

2. **Develop a Resilience Plan**: Work with children to develop a "resilience plan" for handling setbacks. This plan could include identifying someone to whom they can talk, activities that help them feel better, and positive affirmations to remind themselves of their strengths.

3. **Role-Play Challenging Situations**: Use role-playing to prepare children for potential setbacks, practicing how to apply resilience and kindness in response. This preparatory exercise can demystify challenges and equip children with strategies for handling them.

Teaching resilience through kindness offers a dual benefit: it equips children with the skills to navigate life's challenges while emphasizing the importance of compassion toward oneself and others. Parents and caregivers can lay a strong foundation for their children's emotional and psychological well-being by modeling resilience, practicing self-kindness, and engaging in mindful, positive practices. As families embark on this journey together, they cultivate a resilient spirit and a kinder, more empathetic approach to life's ups and downs.

Kindness in Conflict Resolution

Conflict is inevitable in human relationships, arising from differences in needs, desires, and perspectives. However, how we navigate these conflicts can significantly impact our relationships and personal growth. Approaching conflict resolution with kindness and empathy facilitates more effective problem-solving, strengthens bonds, and fosters mutual respect. This section explores actionable techniques for resolving conflicts compassionately, offering scripts and strategies designed to de-escalate tension and find solutions that honor everyone's needs.

The Foundation: Empathy and Compassionate Communication

Empathy, the ability to understand and share another person's feelings, is the cornerstone of resolving conflicts with kindness. It allows us to see beyond our perspective and consider the emotions and needs driving the other person's behavior. Compassionate communication—rooted in empathy—focuses on expressing our needs and feelings without assigning blame, creating a safe space for open dialogue.

Let's look at a high-level overview of a process for navigating a conflict from its initial "blowup" to a resolution. Following the overview are several conflict resolution scripts that deal with situations many of us might encounter regularly.

General Script for Compassionate Communication:

1. **Start with a Positive Intent**: "I value our relationship and want to understand your perspective better."

2. **Express Your Feelings Using "I" Statements**: "I feel [emotion] when [specific situation] because it makes me need/want [specific need]."

3. **Invite the Other Person's Perspective**: "Can you share how you feel about this situation?"

4. **Seek Common Ground**: "Let's find a way forward that meets both our needs."

Techniques for De-escalating Tension

De-escalation is crucial in preventing conflicts from escalating into more significant disputes. Techniques include:

- **Active Listening**: Show that you're listening by nodding, maintaining eye contact, and summarizing the other person's points to affirm you understand their perspective.

- **Maintain Calm Body Language**: Use open gestures, avoid crossing arms, and maintain a relaxed posture to convey openness and reduce defensiveness.

- **Use Humor (When Appropriate)**: Light-hearted humor can relieve tension, but be sensitive to the context and ensure it's not at the other's expense.

Finding Win-Win Solutions

A win-win solution is one where all parties feel their needs are respected and met. Achieving this requires creativity, flexibility, and a commitment to mutual benefit.

- **Brainstorm Together**: Encourage all parties to suggest solutions, focusing on ideas that address the underlying needs rather than the initial positions.

- **Evaluate Options Together**: Discuss the pros and cons of each suggestion, considering how well they meet everyone's needs.

- **Agree on a Solution**: Choose the option that best satisfies all parties and make a plan for implementing it.

Emphasizing Empathy in Understanding All Sides

Understanding all sides of a conflict involves a deep empathy that acknowledges each person's feelings and needs. Techniques include:

- **Reflective Listening**: Paraphrase what the other person has said to show you're trying to understand their perspective deeply.

- **Ask Open-Ended Questions**: Encourage elaboration and clarification, which can reveal underlying needs and feelings.

- **Acknowledge Emotions**: Recognize and validate the emotions involved, even if you disagree with the other person's viewpoint.

Specific Scripts for Compassionate Communication

So, let's get into some specifics, where the rubber meets the road. Below are several specific situations that many parents and caregivers encounter regularly, broken down by age group: young children (ages 3-7), school-aged children (8-12), and teenagers (13-17). Each script is designed to guide children through expressing themselves kindly and understanding others, even in the simplest of conflicts, considering the nuances of each age group.

Young Children (Ages 3 to 7)

Expanding on the script for compassionate communication, here are three tailored scenarios for young children ages 3 to 7. Each script is designed to help children express themselves kindly and understand others, even in the simplest of conflicts. With a bit of coaching and direction, don't underestimate even the youngest of these children to handle themselves well in these kinds of scenarios!

Scenario 1: Toy Sharing Dispute

Situation: Two children want to play with the same toy truck, leading to a disagreement.

Script:

1. **Start with a Positive Intent**: "I know we both love playing with the truck, and I enjoy playing with you."

2. **Express Your Feelings Using "I" Statements**: "I feel sad when we can't share the truck because I want us both to have fun playing together."

3. **Invite the Other Person's Perspective**: "How do you feel when we both want to play with the same toy at the same time?"

4. **Seek Common Ground**: "Let's find a way for both of us to get a turn. Maybe we can set a timer for each of us to play with the truck or find another fun game we can play together afterward."

Scenario 2: Clean-Up Time Conflict

Situation: One child feels overwhelmed by the mess and doesn't want to start cleaning up, while the other is ready to clean.

Script:

1. **Start with a Positive Intent**: "Cleaning up together means we can play more games afterward, and I love spending time with you."

2. **Express Your Feelings Using "I" Statements**: "I feel worried when we have a lot to clean because I think it might take too long, and I want to make sure we have time to read our favorite book together."

3. **Invite the Other Person's Perspective**: "How do you feel about cleaning up right now? Is there something specific you'd like to do after we're done?"

4. **Seek Common Ground**: "Let's make cleaning up a game and see if we can beat the clock! Afterward, we can choose a special activity to do together. What would you like that to be?"

Scenario 3: Bedtime Resistance

Situation: A child doesn't want to go to bed, feeling upset about ending playtime.

Script:

1. **Start with a Positive Intent**: "I love our playtime together, too, and getting enough sleep is how we make sure we're ready for more fun tomorrow."

2. **Express Your Feelings Using "I" Statements**: "I feel concerned when bedtime is hard because I know how important sleep is for

us to have energy. I want to make sure you're rested and happy."

3. **Invite the Other Person's Perspective**: "What makes bedtime feel hard for you? Is there something specific that would make it easier?"

4. **Seek Common Ground**: "Let's create a cozy bedtime routine that we both enjoy. Maybe we can choose a bedtime story to read together or pick out a special stuffed animal to take to bed. What sounds good to you?"

These scenarios, framed with compassionate communication, aim to teach young children the value of expressing their emotions positively and considering others' feelings. By practicing these scripts, children can learn to navigate conflicts with empathy, laying the groundwork for kind and understanding interactions.

School-aged children (Ages 8-12)

For school-aged children, navigating conflicts and expressing emotions require a nuanced understanding of empathy and the ability to articulate feelings and needs. Here are three expanded scenarios for children aged 8 to 12, demonstrating how to apply the script for compassionate communication in various situations.

Scenario 1: Group Project Disagreements

Situation: A disagreement arises in a group project about who should do what part of the assignment.

Script:

1. **Start with a Positive Intent**: "I really value everyone's input in our project, and I believe we can create something amazing together."

2. **Express Your Feelings Using "I" Statements**: "I feel frustrated when we can't decide on our roles because I'm worried we won't finish on time. I want us to work efficiently and fairly."

3. **Invite the Other Person's Perspective**: "What are your thoughts about the project and our roles? Is there a part you're particularly excited about or feel skilled at doing?"

4. **Seek Common Ground**: "Let's each talk about our strengths and interests and see if we can assign roles that play to our strengths. This way, we all contribute meaningfully and complete our project successfully."

Scenario 2: Exclusion from Play

Situation: A child feels left out when their friends decide to play a game without inviting them.

Script:

1. **Start with a Positive Intent**: "I enjoy spending time with you all and playing together. It's important to me that we have fun as a group."

2. **Express Your Feelings Using "I" Statements**: "I feel hurt when I'm not included in the game because it makes me feel left out. I want to be part of our group activities and enjoy our time together."

3. **Invite the Other Person's Perspective**: "Was there a reason I wasn't included this time? I'd like to understand if there's something I should know."

4. **Seek Common Ground**: "Let's find a game we all enjoy and can play together. Or, if there are too many of us for one game, we can take turns or split into teams. What do you think?"

Scenario 3: Misunderstanding with a Friend

Situation: A misunderstanding leads to a conflict between two friends over something said that was taken out of context.

Script:

1. **Start with a Positive Intent**: "Our friendship means a lot to me, and I want to clear up any misunderstanding so we can move past this."

2. **Express Your Feelings Using "I" Statements**: "I feel upset about our disagreement because it seems like my words were misunderstood. I need us to communicate openly so we can resolve this."

3. **Invite the Other Person's Perspective**: "Can you share how you interpreted what I said and how it made you feel? I want to understand your perspective."

4. **Seek Common Ground**: "Let's both share what we meant and how we felt without blaming each other. From there, we can figure out how to avoid similar misunderstandings in the future and strengthen our friendship."

These scripts offer a framework for school-aged children to approach conflicts with empathy and a desire for mutual understanding. By practicing compassionate communication, children can learn to navigate disagreements constructively, fostering stronger relationships and a deeper understanding of others.

Teenagers (Ages 13-17)

Compassionate communication is vital to resolving conflicts and building understanding for teenagers navigating the complexities of relationships and personal identity. Here are three scenarios tailored for teenagers (ages 13-17), demonstrating how to effectively apply the script for compassionate communication.

Scenario 1: Social Media Misunderstanding

Situation: A post on social media leads to a misunderstanding among friends, with feelings hurt and intentions questioned.

Script:

1. **Start with a Positive Intent**: "I really value our friendship, and I believe it's important we understand each other clearly, especially on sensitive topics."

2. **Express Your Feelings Using "I" Statements**: "I feel upset about the post because it seemed to send a message that wasn't intended. I need to clarify my intentions and understand how it came across to you."

3. **Invite the Other Person's Perspective**: "How did you interpret the post, and how did it make you feel? I want to understand your viewpoint so we can move past this together."

4. **Seek Common Ground**: "Let's discuss how we can use social media to strengthen our friendship rather than cause misunderstandings. Maybe we can agree to communicate directly if something bothers us before assuming the worst."

Scenario 2: Disagreement Over Family Responsibilities

Situation: Tension arises between teenagers and their parents over perceived unfairness in the distribution of household chores.

Script:

1. **Start with a Positive Intent**: "I know we all contribute to our home, and I want us to feel that contributions are fair and valued."

2. **Express Your Feelings Using "I" Statements**: "I feel frustrated when asked to do more chores than my siblings because it seems unfair. I need to feel that there's a balance in our responsibilities."

3. **Invite the Other Person's Perspective**: "How do you decide who does what chores? I'm interested in understanding your approach and discussing how we feel about it."

4. **Seek Common Ground**: "Can we create a schedule or system that considers each person's activities and fairness in chores? I think working on this together could help us all feel more satisfied and understood."

Scenario 3: Peer Pressure and Personal Values

Situation: A teenager feels pressured by friends to engage in activities that conflict with their values and beliefs.

Script:

1. **Start with a Positive Intent**: "I really appreciate our friendship and the times we share, and I think it's important we respect each other's beliefs and boundaries."

2. **Express Your Feelings Using "I" Statements**: "I feel uncomfortable when there's pressure to participate in things that go against my values. I must stay true to myself, even though I want to fit in with our group."

3. **Invite the Other Person's Perspective**: "How do you feel about these activities, and do you think there's room for us to have fun together without compromising our personal values?"

4. **Seek Common Ground**: "Let's find activities we all enjoy and that don't make anyone feel compromised. I believe there's plenty we can do that aligns with everyone's comfort zone and values."

Resolving conflicts with kindness and empathy is a powerful approach that transforms challenges into opportunities for growth and connection. By practicing compassionate communication, de-escalating tension, and seeking win-win solutions, we can navigate disagreements in ways that strengthen relationships rather than weaken them. The scripts and strategies provided here are starting points, inviting individuals and families to adapt and expand upon them in ways that resonate with their unique situations and relationships. Ultimately, kindness in conflict resolution is about honoring our shared humanity and recognizing that empathy and understanding are the keys to finding resolutions that uplift and unite us.

Learning from Mistakes with a Kind Heart

A young boy named Leo lived in the quaint town of Willow Creek, nestled between rolling hills and whispering forests. Leo, with his boundless curiosity and zest for life, was known for his adventurous spirit. However, with great adventures often came great mistakes, and Leo was no stranger to them. From a science project that bubbled over in spectacular fashion to a misguided attempt at repairing his father's watch, Leo's endeavors sometimes went differently than planned.

One day, Leo decided to build a birdhouse for his backyard, hoping to give the local birds a place to call home. Despite his enthusiasm, his first attempt could have been more successful. The birdhouse was lopsided, the door too small, and it fell apart at the slightest touch. Disheartened, Leo was ready to abandon his project, weighed down by the heavy cloak of failure.

It was then that his grandmother, Mia, a retired school teacher with a gentle smile and eyes that sparkled with wisdom, sat beside him. Mia, who had observed Leo's frustration, saw an invaluable teaching moment in the ruins of the wooden birdhouse.

"Leo, do you know what makes a wise person?" she asked, her voice soft yet clear.

"No, what?" Leo responded with his curiosity piqued despite his disappointment.

"A wise person isn't someone who never makes mistakes. They are someone who learns from them," Mia explained. "Each mistake is a stepping stone to something greater, not a reason to stop trying."

Together, they examined the remains of the birdhouse. Mia pointed out what might have gone wrong and asked Leo how he might approach it differently next time. Encouraged by his grandmother's kindness and lack of judgment, Leo began to see his failed attempt not as a defeat but as a learning opportunity.

With renewed determination, Leo set out to build another birdhouse, applying the lessons learned from his previous mistakes. This time, the birdhouse stood firm and welcoming, a testament to Leo's growth and perseverance.

Through this experience, Leo discovered the power of a growth mindset. He learned that embracing mistakes as opportunities for learning allowed him to extend kindness to himself and others. He became more patient and understanding, recognizing that everyone, at some point, faces setbacks and challenges. Leo's journey with the birdhouse became a story he shared often, inspiring a culture of continuous improvement and forgiveness among his friends and family.

This tale of Leo and the birdhouse illustrates the transformative potential of viewing mistakes through the lens of kindness and growth. By learning to approach errors without self-judgment, we open ourselves to the endless possibilities of personal development and collective betterment. Doing so fosters a kinder, more compassionate world where each mistake is a gateway to greater wisdom and resilience.

Remember our lesson from Chapter 1: "Learn from Faux Pas." Leo's story illustrates that the journey of learning from our mistakes, guided by a kind heart and a growth mindset, is a profound source of personal and communal enrichment. I encourage you to embrace your imperfections, forgive yourself and others, and move forward, knowing that every misstep brings you closer to the person you were created to be.

Reflective Conclusion

As we've seen, kindness is not merely a soft glow in the gentle moments of life but a profound source of light and strength in times of darkness and difficulty. It teaches us that resilience is not about the absence of vulnerability but about facing our struggles with courage, compassion, and an open heart. By leading with kindness, we not only navigate our challenges more effectively but also model how to do the same for our children.

As parents and caregivers, we bear the mantle of leadership not as a burden but as a privilege. We have the unique opportunity to shape the hearts and minds of the next generation, to sow seeds of empathy, understanding, and resilience that will grow into a forest of kindness. This responsibility begins with our actions and the choices we make in moments, both big and small.

To reinforce the messages of this chapter and encourage continuous reflection and growth, consider these questions:

1. **How do I demonstrate kindness in the face of my own challenges?** Reflect on how you

model resilience through kindness, showing your children that it is a source of strength.

2. **What opportunities can I find in everyday adversities to teach kindness and empathy?** Think about your daily challenges and how they can serve as teachable moments for your children.

3. **How can I foster an environment where kindness is seen as a foundational value?** Consider the steps you can take to cultivate a family culture that prioritizes kindness in all interactions.

4. **In what ways can I encourage my children to see kindness as a tool for overcoming adversity?** Reflect on strategies to help your children understand that kindness can be their compass in navigating life's challenges.

Remember, kindness is not a sign of weakness but a profound source of strength and resilience. By leading with kindness, we overcome our adversities and empower our children to do the same, paving the way for a future marked by compassion, understanding, and unwavering strength.

Chapter 6:
Cultivating a Kindness Mindset for Life

You cannot do kindness too soon, for you never know how soon it will be too late. –Ralph Waldo Emerson

Kindness in words creates confidence. Kindness in thinking creates profoundness. Kindness in giving creates love. –Lao Tzu

The best way to find yourself is to lose yourself in the service of others. –Mahatma Gandhi

The Kindness Mindset

Let's dive into what it means to foster a mentality where kindness is not merely an act performed but a foundational principle that guides our lives. First, we'll define the concept of a kindness mindset and then explore its profound significance on both personal and societal levels, highlighting how such a perspective shapes our decision-making, relationships, and journey of personal growth.

What is a Kindness Mindset?

A kindness mindset is an ingrained attitude that prioritizes compassion, empathy, and kindness in every aspect of life. It's a way of seeing and interacting with the world that elevates kindness to a guiding principle, influencing how we treat others, navigate challenges, and make choices. This mindset isn't limited to grand gestures; it encompasses the small, everyday actions and decisions that collectively define the character of our lives and communities.

The Significance of a Kindness Mindset

The significance of adopting a kindness mindset extends far beyond the immediate benefits to ourselves and those with whom we directly interact. It's a transformative force that impacts society, fostering environments where empathy, understanding, and mutual respect flourish. Kindness begets kindness; it creates a positive feedback loop that enhances the well-being of individuals and communities alike.

A kindness mindset is a powerful catalyst for personal growth. It encourages individuals to approach challenges with compassion, not only toward others but also themselves. This gentle, empathetic approach to problem-solving and personal development fosters resilience, reduces stress, and promotes a healthier, more fulfilling life.

Influence on Decision-Making and Relationships

At the heart of a kindness mindset is its influence on our decision-making processes. Decisions informed by kindness consider the well-being of others and our own, leading to more inclusive, thoughtful, and beneficial choices in the long term. This approach enhances personal integrity and builds trust, laying a solid foundation for positive relationships in all areas of life.

A kindness mindset acts as a bridge in relationships, connecting individuals through a shared commitment to compassion and understanding. It nurtures deeper connections, facilitates open and honest communication, and creates a safe space for vulnerability. These qualities are essential for building strong, supportive relationships that withstand the tests of time and challenge.

Psychological Research and Expert Opinions

The benefits of a kindness-oriented approach to life are well-documented in psychological research. Acts of kindness release endorphins, promoting happiness and reducing stress both for the giver and the receiver (Post, 2011). Studies by Dr. Sonja Lyubomirsky, a professor of psychology at the University of California, Riverside, have shown that performing acts of kindness can increase well-being and happiness. The research suggests that kind acts contribute to the giver's happiness in a significant way, supporting the idea that kindness is beneficial for both the giver and the receiver (Layous, 2017).

Moreover, kindness has been linked to improved health outcomes, including lower blood pressure and increased lifespan (Shobitha & Kohli, 2015; Fritz, 2019).

Experts in psychology and behavioral science, such as Dr. Richard Davidson, emphasize the neural basis for kindness and compassion (Lutz et al., 2008). According to Davidson, kindness is not just a moral virtue but a skill that can be cultivated, profoundly affecting our brain's structure and function. This neuroplasticity underscores the potential for a kindness mindset to bring about lasting change in individuals and society.

The Kindness Mindset as a Gift and Responsibility

Cultivating a kindness mindset is both a gift and a responsibility. It's a gift that enriches our lives, enhancing our capacity for joy, satisfaction, and connection. Simultaneously, we are responsible for nurturing and spreading kindness, impacting the world in tangible, positive ways. Parents and caregivers play a crucial role in this process, as they have the unique opportunity to instill a kindness mindset in their children from a young age.

By modeling kindness, encouraging empathetic understanding, and fostering an environment where kindness is valued and practiced, parents can lay the groundwork for their children to develop a kindness mindset. This foundation benefits the children's personal growth and relationships and creates a more compassionate, understanding society.

As we delve deeper into cultivating a kindness mindset for life, it's clear that the implications of such a perspective are far-reaching. A kindness mindset is a profound source of personal and social transformation that influences everything from our daily decisions to our most cherished relationships. Throughout this chapter, we will explore practical strategies and insights for nurturing this mindset, ensuring that kindness becomes a steadfast companion in our journey through life.

Daily Practices

Cultivating a kindness mindset is a journey that begins with the intentional integration of simple, daily practices into our lives. When repeated over time, these practices reinforce the value of kindness and weave it into the fabric of our daily existence. For families looking to foster this mindset, incorporating specific rituals and habits can be particularly effective, offering a roadmap for living more compassionately.

Starting the Day with Kind Intentions

1. **Morning Kindness Circle**: Begin each day with a family kindness circle where each member shares a kind intention for the day. This could be something as simple as smiling at a stranger, offering help without being asked, or expressing gratitude to a teacher or colleague. For younger children, intentions might focus on sharing, using polite words, or helping with a household chore. Teenagers might set intentions related to supporting a friend or advocating for positive change in their community.

2. **Kindness Affirmations**: Create a set of kindness affirmations from which family members can choose or recite together each morning. These affirmations can serve as reminders of the importance of kindness throughout the day. Examples include "I choose kindness in every interaction today" or "I am a source of kindness and light."

Recognizing Opportunities for Kindness in Everyday Moments

1. **Kindness Spotting**: Challenge each family member to "spot" acts of kindness throughout their day, whether performed by themselves or

others. During dinner or evening family time, share these observations, discussing the impact of these acts on both the giver and receiver. This practice helps children and adults alike become more aware of the presence of kindness in everyday life and its power to transform ordinary moments.

2. **Random Acts of Kindness**: Encourage spontaneous acts of kindness by keeping a "kindness kit" ready. This could include small notes of encouragement, art supplies for making greeting cards, or small tokens to give away. Children can be involved in preparing these items and deciding how to use them to surprise friends, family members, or even strangers.

Ending the Day with Reflection on Kind Acts

1. **Kindness Journal**: Maintain a family kindness journal where each member can record the kind acts they performed, witnessed, or received during the day. This reflective practice allows the family to end the day positively, reinforcing the idea that kindness is both impactful and rewarding.

2. **Gratitude and Kindness Reflection**: Before bedtime, encourage a moment of reflection on

the day's events, focusing specifically on moments of gratitude and acts of kindness. Depending on each family member's age and preference, this can be a quiet, individual practice or a shared family activity. For younger children, discuss the kind acts in the form of stories to help them connect emotionally with the practice of kindness.

Adapting Practices for Different Ages and Stages of Development

1. **For Young Children**: Emphasize kindness through play and storytelling, using puppets or toys to act out kind behaviors. Encourage simple, age-appropriate acts of kindness, like drawing a picture for a family member or sharing toys with friends.

2. **For School-Aged Children**: Focus on empathy-building activities, like discussing the feelings and perspectives of characters in books or movies. Encourage them to take on small responsibilities that contribute to the family or community, such as caring for a pet or helping to prepare a meal.

3. **For Teenagers**: Discuss broader social issues and explore how acts of kindness can help address these challenges. Support their

involvement in community service or social justice initiatives that align with their interests and values.

By integrating these daily practices into family life, parents and caregivers can significantly impact nurturing a kindness mindset among all family members. These rituals, tailored to meet the developmental needs of children at different stages, not only reinforce the importance of kindness as a daily practice but also strengthen the bonds within the family and extend a ripple of compassion into the wider community. As these practices become ingrained habits, they lay the foundation for a life characterized by kindness, empathy, and a deep commitment to positive change.

Positive Reinforcement

Positive reinforcement is a cornerstone concept in behavioral psychology. It involves introducing a rewarding stimulus following a desired behavior, which increases the likelihood of the behavior being repeated. Positive reinforcement can significantly enhance children's inclination to act kindly by associating such behavior with positive outcomes when applied to fostering kindness in children.

The Role of Praise in Reinforcing Kindness

Praising children for acts of kindness is a powerful form of positive reinforcement. However, the key to effective praise is focusing on the action and the intention and effort behind it. This nuanced approach ensures that children understand that not just the act of kindness but also the empathetic and thoughtful mindset that prompted it is valued.

1. **Be Specific in Your Praise**: Instead of general comments like "Good job," specify what was good about the action. For example, "I noticed you helped your brother with homework without being asked. That was very thoughtful and kind."

2. **Acknowledge the Effort**: Recognize the effort involved, especially if the act of kindness required overcoming challenges or putting significant thought into someone else's needs. "I know it wasn't easy to give up some of your playtime to help out, and I'm really proud of the choice you made."

3. **Praise the Thought Behind the Act**: Highlight the thought process and empathy behind the kind act. "It was very kind of you to think about how your friend might feel lonely. Inviting them to join our game was a lovely way to show you care."

Balancing Praise and Rewards

While praise effectively reinforces kindness, introducing tangible rewards requires careful consideration to avoid making kindness seem transactional. The goal is to encourage children to value kindness as its own reward rather than something they perform expecting external rewards.

1. **Use Tangible Rewards Sparingly**: Reserve tangible rewards for exceptional acts of kindness or behavior milestones to maintain their effectiveness and ensure that acts of kindness are not performed solely for rewards.

2. **Focus on Intrinsic Rewards**: Emphasize the positive feelings that come from being kind, such as happiness, satisfaction, and a sense of connection with others. Encourage children to reflect on how their kind acts made them feel internally, reinforcing the intrinsic value of kindness.

3. **Create a Culture of Kindness**: Foster an environment where kindness is expected and celebrated in daily life. This can involve setting family kindness goals, sharing stories of kindness at mealtimes, and modeling kindness in your interactions.

Encouraging a Kindness Mindset Beyond Acts

Fostering a kindness mindset involves reinforcing the understanding that kindness is a way of life, not just a series of actions. Encourage children to consider how they can incorporate kindness into their thoughts and attitudes, as well as their actions.

1. **Discuss Kind Thoughts**: Have conversations about kind thoughts and attitudes and how they can influence actions. Encourage children to think kindly about themselves and others, even in challenging situations.

2. **Model Kindness in Thought and Action**: Demonstrate how you incorporate kindness into your own life, not just through actions but also in how you speak about and think of others. This modeling provides a powerful example for children to emulate.

When applied thoughtfully, positive reinforcement is a powerful tool in cultivating a kindness mindset in children. By focusing praise on the intention, effort, and thought behind kind acts and maintaining a balance between praise and rewards, parents and caregivers can foster a genuine appreciation for kindness. Encouraging children to value the intrinsic rewards of kindness ensures their motivation remains focused on the joy and fulfillment of empathetic and compassionate behavior. Through these practices, we can nurture a generation that views kindness not as an obligation but as a fundamental, rewarding aspect of their lives.

Kindness as a Family Value

Integrating kindness into the essence of family life transforms it from a mere behavior into a core value akin to honesty or hard work. This deep embedding of kindness fosters an environment where compassion, empathy, and caring interactions become the norm, influencing every family member's development and worldview. Let's outline strategies and suggest rituals to help families celebrate and prioritize kindness as a foundational value.

Establishing Kindness as a Core Family Value

1. **Family Mission Statement**: Collaboratively craft a family mission statement that includes kindness as a central value. This activity allows each family member to contribute their understanding and importance of kindness, solidifying its role in your collective lives.

2. **Kindness Story Time**: Dedicate weekly time for family members to share stories from their lives or history that exemplify kindness. These can be personal experiences, historical anecdotes, or stories from literature. This ritual highlights the impact of kindness and strengthens family bonds through shared narratives.

Celebrating Kindness in Daily Life

1. **Daily Kindness Check-ins**: Incorporate kindness into daily conversations by asking family members to share an act of kindness they performed, witnessed, or received that day. This can be part of dinner time or bedtime routines, fostering a daily reflection on the importance of kindness.

2. **Kindness Board**: Create a central place in your home, like a bulletin board or a digital platform for older children, where family members can post notes about acts of kindness. This visible reminder will constantly inspire and celebrate kind actions within and outside the family.

Embedding Kindness Through Rituals and Traditions

1. **Monthly Kindness Projects**: Organize a family kindness project each month, such as volunteering at a local shelter, making care packages for people experiencing homelessness, or writing letters to elderly residents in nursing homes. Rotating the project focus allows for exploring various ways to express kindness, teaching children its multifaceted nature.

2. **Kindness Advent Calendar**: Adapt the advent calendar tradition to focus on kindness in the lead-up to significant family celebrations or holidays. Each day can reveal a new act of kindness to perform, turning anticipation into action.

3. **Kindness Awards**: Hold a monthly or quarterly "kindness awards" night where family members acknowledge and celebrate specific acts of kindness each has demonstrated. This can be as simple as verbal recognition or involve symbolic tokens of appreciation.

Strategies for Sustaining Kindness as a Family Value

1. **Modeling Kindness**: Parents and caregivers should lead by example, consistently demonstrating kindness in actions, words, and decision-making. This consistent modeling reinforces kindness as a way of life, not just an expectation for the younger members. (Am I that broken record on this point yet?)

2. **Kindness in Conflict Resolution**: Use family disagreements as opportunities to practice kindness, emphasizing understanding and empathy and finding solutions that honor

everyone's feelings and needs. This approach teaches that kindness is crucial, especially in challenging situations.

3. **Feedback and Reflection**: Regularly reflect as a family on how well you are living up to your kindness value. Openly discuss challenges and successes and encourage honest feedback on ways to improve. This ongoing reflection ensures that kindness remains a dynamic and evolving part of family life.

Making kindness a fundamental family value is a journey that requires intention, practice, and dedication. By establishing rituals and traditions that celebrate and prioritize kindness, families can create a culture where compassion and empathy are as ingrained as honesty and hard work. These practices enhance the family unit and extend their impact outward, contributing to a kinder, more empathetic world. Through daily acts of kindness, celebrating kindness achievements, and embedding kindness into the fabric of family life, we can nurture a legacy of compassion that will influence future generations.

Practical Tips

Cultivating a kindness mindset is an enriching but sometimes challenging journey. Families may encounter obstacles, such as unkind behavior from others or societal pressures that value competition over cooperation. Overcoming these challenges requires intentionality, resilience, and strategies that reinforce the importance of kindness even under challenging circumstances.

Dealing with Unkind Behavior

1. **Modeling Empathy**: When faced with unkind behavior, model empathy by trying to understand the reasons behind the behavior. Discuss with your family that often, unkindness stems from hurt, fear, or misunderstanding. Encourage a response that seeks to understand rather than retaliate.

2. **Teaching Assertive Communication**: Equip your family with the skills to express their feelings and boundaries assertively, not aggressively, in the face of unkind behavior. Phrases like, "I feel hurt when you say things like that, and I would appreciate it if you didn't," empower individuals to stand up for themselves kindly and respectfully.

3. **Practicing Forgiveness**: Foster an environment where forgiveness is valued as a strength. Discuss the power of letting go of grudges for personal peace and model forgiveness in your

actions. Highlight that forgiving does not mean condoning unkind behavior but freeing oneself from ongoing negativity.

Navigating Societal Pressures

1. **Encouraging Cooperative Play and Activities**: In a world that often glorifies competition, make a conscious effort to engage in cooperative games and activities that require teamwork and collaboration. Discuss the joy and satisfaction derived from working together toward a common goal.

2. **Critical Consumption of Media**: Together, critically assess media that glorifies competitive over cooperative behavior. Encourage discussions about the underlying messages and brainstorm ways to counteract these with examples of kindness and cooperation from your lives or history.

3. **Celebrating Acts of Kindness Over Wins**: Shift the focus from winning to kindness by celebrating acts of kindness just as much, if not more, than achievements. Share stories of kindness heroes in society, and recognize family members when they demonstrate kindness, especially in challenging situations.

Building Resilience in Kindness

1. **Kindness Reflections**: Incorporate regular reflections on acts of kindness experienced, performed, or observed. Discussing these moments reinforces the belief in kindness as a source of strength and resilience.

2. **Role-playing Challenges**: Prepare for potential challenges by role-playing situations where maintaining a kindness mindset might be difficult. This preparation can help family members feel more confident in navigating these situations in real life.

3. **Support Systems**: Build a support system of like-minded families and individuals who value kindness. Being part of a community that shares your values can provide encouragement and inspiration when challenges arise.

Maintaining a Kindness Mindset

1. **Continual Learning**: Encourage a growth and learning mindset, where maintaining kindness is seen as an ongoing journey. Explore books, workshops, and other resources on kindness, empathy, and compassion together as a family.

2. **Mindfulness and Self-Compassion Practices**: Integrate mindfulness and self-compassion practices into your routine. These can help manage reactions to unkind behavior and societal pressures, reinforcing a kindness mindset when facing challenges.

3. **Setting Kindness Goals**: Set personal and family goals related to kindness, such as performing a certain number of kind acts each month or learning about and supporting a new charitable cause. Reflect on these goals regularly to track progress and adjust as needed.

Maintaining a kindness mindset amidst challenges is a testament to a family's commitment to fostering a more compassionate world. Families can gracefully navigate the complexities of unkind behavior and societal pressures by modeling empathy, teaching assertive communication, practicing forgiveness, and building resilience. Encouraging cooperative behaviors, critically consuming media, and celebrating acts of kindness are vital strategies for reinforcing kindness as a fundamental value. Through continual learning, support systems, and mindfulness, cultivating a kindness mindset becomes an enriching path for personal growth and societal contribution.

Reflective Conclusion

As we conclude this chapter, it's time to turn inward and reflect on our journey toward embedding kindness into the essence of our being and family life.

This chapter has explored the transformative power of kindness, not just as a series of actions but as a profound mindset that shapes our decisions, relationships, and impact on the world. This is your call to action, a moment to commit to kindness as a practice and a lifelong journey of growth and connection.

Reflective Questions

1. **How do I currently embody a kindness mindset in my daily life?** Reflect on the moments when kindness guides your actions and decisions. Consider both the easy and challenging times to be kind.

2. **In what situations do I find it most difficult to maintain a kindness mindset?** Identifying

these challenges is the first step toward overcoming them. Consider why these situations are difficult and what might help you respond with kindness.

3. **How does my behavior model a kindness mindset to others, especially children?** Children learn by example. Reflect on how your actions and words teach kindness, even subtly.

4. **What barriers to kindness do I observe in myself, my family, or my community?** Recognizing these barriers can help you understand the changes needed to foster a more kindness-oriented environment.

Prompts for Setting Goals

1. **Personal Kindness Goals:** Set specific, achievable goals for yourself that reflect a commitment to growing your kindness mindset. This could involve daily acts of kindness, adopting a new mindfulness practice to enhance empathy, or learning more about cultures and experiences different from your own to broaden your understanding and compassion.

2. **Family Kindness Goals:** Collaboratively identify goals your family can work toward

together. This might include regular volunteer work, starting a kindness project based on interests or talents, or establishing a family kindness ritual, such as a weekly reflection on acts of kindness observed or performed.

3. **Challenges to Overcome:** Based on the difficulties you identified earlier, set goals to address these challenges. If, for example, you struggle with kindness in moments of stress, your goal could be to develop and practice stress-reduction techniques or to pause and take three deep breaths before responding to challenging situations.

4. **Kindness as a Response to Unkindness:** Consider how you can commit to responding with kindness even when faced with unkindness. This might involve role-playing responses to unkind actions or words to prepare yourself and your family to respond with compassion and understanding.

This reflection and goal-setting process is your commitment to making kindness a defining value in your and your family's lives. Please write down your goals and the steps you plan to take to achieve them. Place them somewhere visible as a daily reminder of your commitment to cultivating a kindness mindset for life.

Kindness is a powerful force that can transform lives and communities. By committing to a kindness mindset, you embark on a journey filled with growth, challenges, and the joy of making a positive impact. Let's let kindness guide our actions, influence our decisions, and shape the legacy we leave behind.

Chapter 7:
Digital Kindness: Navigating the Online World

Speak to everyone with kindness, even on the internet.
  –Germany Kent

In a world where you can be anything, be kind.
  –Jennifer Dukes Lee

A little consideration, a little thought for others, makes all the difference. –Eeyore, Winnie the Pooh by A.A. Milne

In the digital age, the online realm has become a pervasive force in our lives, particularly for children and teenagers. This digital landscape offers vast opportunities for learning, connecting, and expressing oneself. However, it also presents unique challenges, notably in interacting with others. The anonymity and distance screens provide can sometimes lead to behaviors that starkly contradict the principles of kindness and empathy.

The digital world is a double-edged sword. On one side, it breaks down barriers, allowing us to connect with diverse communities and share moments of compassion and understanding on an unimaginable scale. On the other hand, it can be a breeding ground for negativity, where unkind words and actions proliferate free from the immediate consequences seen in face-to-face interactions. This dichotomy poses a significant challenge for parents and caregivers striving to instill values of kindness and empathy in their children.

Our thoughts here will underscore the importance of parental involvement in guiding and supporting children's online activities. The aim is to equip parents and caregivers with tools to guide their children through the digital world with kindness at the forefront. Through practical advice and thoughtful discussion, children and teenagers can be prepared to navigate the digital realm safely and contribute to making it a kinder, more inclusive space for all.

Understanding the Impact of Cyberbullying

In navigating the complexities of our digital world, understanding cyberbullying is paramount for parents and caregivers aiming to cultivate a kindness mindset in children and teenagers. This section delves into the nuances of cyberbullying, its impacts, and strategies for prevention and response, providing a comprehensive guide to tackling one of the digital age's most pressing challenges.

Defining Cyberbullying

Cyberbullying is any form of bullying that takes place over digital devices like computers, tablets, and smartphones. It encompasses sending, posting, or sharing negative, harmful, false, or mean content about someone else, often leading to embarrassment or humiliation. Unlike traditional bullying, which requires face-to-face interaction, cyberbullying can occur through text messaging and apps or online social media, forums, or gaming, where people can view, participate in, or share content.

A critical aspect that differentiates cyberbullying from traditional forms is the anonymity the internet can provide. This anonymity can embolden individuals to engage in more severe forms of bullying, believing they are insulated from the consequences of their actions. This faceless nature often amplifies the emotional toll on the victim, making it a uniquely distressing experience.

Consequences of Cyberbullying

The impact of cyberbullying on children and teenagers can be profound, affecting their psychological, emotional, and sometimes physical well-being. Victims may experience increased anxiety, depression, and loneliness, leading to significant distress and, in severe cases, to self-harm or suicidal ideation. The public and permanent nature of online harassment can intensify these feelings, as the content can be difficult to erase and potentially seen by a large audience.

Recognizing the signs of cyberbullying is crucial. These may include sudden changes in behavior or mood, reluctance to use electronic devices, unexplained anger or depression after going online, and withdrawal from friends and family. Early detection allows for timely intervention, potentially mitigating the adverse effects on the child or teenager's mental and emotional health.

Prevention and Response Strategies

Preventing cyberbullying and responding effectively when it occurs requires a multifaceted approach. Here are some strategies for parents:

1. **Foster Open Communication**: Create an environment where children feel comfortable discussing their online experiences and concerns. Regular conversations about online life can help parents identify potential issues early on.

2. **Educate About Digital Citizenship**: Teach children and teenagers about the responsibilities that come with digital interactions. Emphasize the importance of respect, empathy, and kindness online, highlighting that words and actions have real consequences.

3. **Set Digital Boundaries**: Establish rules for digital device use, including what sites can be visited and what kind of information should not be shared online. Use parental controls where

necessary to monitor and protect your child's online activity.

4. **Encourage Positive Online Interactions**: Guide children to use the internet for positive interactions, such as connecting with friends and family, learning new skills, and sharing kindness.

5. **Know When and How to Intervene**: If cyberbullying occurs, document the abusive content, block the bully on all platforms, and report the behavior to the social media site or app. If the bullying involves threats of violence or other criminal behavior, report it to the authorities. For school-related cyberbullying, contact the school to discuss how they can support your child and address the situation.

6. **Seek Professional Support**: Consider seeking support from a counselor or psychologist if your child shows signs of distress. Professional help can provide coping strategies and emotional support to navigate the effects of cyberbullying.

By understanding cyberbullying and implementing these strategies, parents and caregivers can protect children and teenagers from its harmful effects and foster resilience and kindness in the face of online adversity. It's about equipping them to survive and thrive, creating a digital landscape where kindness prevails.

Promoting Empathy in Digital Communications

Teaching empathy in the context of online interactions is crucial for fostering kind and respectful communication. This section explores the importance of empathy in the digital realm, focusing on how parents can guide their children to navigate online spaces thoughtfully and considerately.

Empathy Online

Digital communication strips away the rich tapestry of non-verbal cues that inform so much of our face-to-face interactions. In this environment, the warmth of a smile, the reassurance of a gentle tone, and the understanding in a nod are lost. This absence makes conveying and interpreting empathy more challenging yet no less important. Teaching children the art of thoughtful online communication is vital to bridge this gap.

Parents can encourage their children to pause before posting or messaging. This pause is a moment to consider their words' weight and reflect on how others might receive them. Questions like, "How would I feel if someone said this to me?" or "Could my words be misunderstood?" can guide children to a more empathetic stance. Encouraging them to imagine the person on the other side of the screen as a friend sitting across from them can help humanize digital interactions.

Understanding Digital Footprints

Every online action leaves a digital footprint, a permanent marker of our online presence. It's essential to discuss with children the lasting nature of what they share and post online. This conversation is an opportunity to emphasize that empathy should be the guiding principle in deciding what to make public. The permanence of online content means that a momentary lapse in judgment can have long-term implications, affecting personal reputation and how others feel.

Parents should encourage open discussions about digital footprints, exploring questions like, "Would I be comfortable with everyone I know seeing this?" or "Could this post negatively impact someone else, now or in the future?" This dialogue can help children understand the lasting impact of their online actions and the importance of empathy in shaping their digital legacy.

Role-Playing and Scenarios

Role-playing exercises and scenarios are practical tools for developing empathy and understanding different perspectives in online interactions. By engaging in role-playing, children can explore various online situations from multiple viewpoints, gaining insight into the feelings and reactions of others.

For example, parents can create scenarios in which one person posts something online that might be hurtful or embarrassing to another, even if unintentionally. Children can better understand the emotional impact of online behaviors by role-playing both the poster's and the recipient's roles. These exercises can cover a range of situations, from cyberbullying to sharing someone else's personal information without consent.

Another approach is to discuss real-life scenarios or news stories related to online interactions, analyzing the perspectives of all involved and exploring alternative, more empathetic responses. This method develops empathy, critical thinking, and digital literacy skills.

Promoting empathy in digital communications is critical to navigating the online world with kindness and respect. By teaching children to consider the feelings of others, understand the permanence of their digital actions, and explore different perspectives through role-playing, parents can cultivate a more empathetic and thoughtful approach to online interactions. These skills are essential for positive digital citizenship and building a kinder, more compassionate digital community.

Being a Positive Influence Online

In an era where digital interactions are often more commonplace than face-to-face conversations, our role in shaping the online atmosphere is more significant than ever. Parents and caregivers can guide their children to navigate the digital world safely and contribute to making it a kinder, more positive space. This involves modeling positive behavior, creating uplifting content, and understanding the responsibilities of digital citizenship.

Modeling Positive Online Behavior

The adage "actions speak louder than words" holds profound truth, especially in the context of digital behavior. Children often emulate the behaviors they observe in adults, making it imperative for parents to demonstrate kindness and positivity in their online interactions. This can include engaging in respectful discussions, sharing positive stories, and offering supportive comments. When children see their parents navigating online disagreements with grace, responding to negativity with understanding, or simply sharing content that brightens someone's day, they learn valuable lessons about digital conduct.

Parents can further this learning by discussing their online interactions with their children, explaining why they chose to respond in specific ways, and how they handle online negativity. This open dialogue reinforces the importance of positive online behavior and prepares children to make kinder choices in their digital interactions.

Creating Positive Content

The content we create and share online has the power to influence not just our immediate circle but the broader digital community. Encouraging children to develop and share content that reflects kindness, positivity, and respect can have a ripple effect, inspiring others to do the same. This can be as simple as sharing stories of personal achievement or acts of kindness, creating art or music that uplifts others, or posting positive comments on social media posts of friends and family members.

Parents can collaborate with their children on projects that contribute to positive online spaces, such as a blog that focuses on family adventures with a kindness twist, a YouTube channel with educational content, or social media accounts that spread positive messages. These activities foster creativity and digital skills and emphasize the impact of positive messaging in building supportive online communities.

Digital Citizenship

Understanding the concept of digital citizenship is crucial for children to appreciate their roles and responsibilities in the online world. This encompasses respecting others' privacy, thinking critically about the accuracy and potential impact of the information they share, and actively avoiding spreading harmful content. Teaching children to be advocates for kindness online is essential to digital citizenship. It involves standing up against cyberbullying, supporting peers who are targeted, and contributing to online environments that discourage negative behaviors.

Parents can teach digital citizenship through discussions about real-world scenarios, guiding children on handling various online situations ethically and kindly. Role-playing exercises can also be practical, allowing children to think through their responses to digital dilemmas. Encouraging children to participate in or initiate online campaigns that promote kindness, understanding, and inclusivity can further solidify their role as positive digital citizens.

Being a positive influence online is a collective effort that starts with individual actions. By modeling positive behavior, creating and sharing uplifting content, and embracing the responsibilities of digital citizenship, parents and children can contribute to making the digital world a kinder, more respectful space. Through mindful digital engagement, we can all play a part in fostering an online environment where kindness prevails.

Navigating Social Media and Online Interactions

In the vast and ever-evolving landscape of social media and online interactions, fostering a navigational compass grounded in kindness, discernment, and respect is crucial. This section aims to equip parents and caregivers with strategies to guide their children in creating and participating in online environments that reflect the values of empathy and integrity.

Setting Boundaries

Establishing healthy boundaries around social media use is foundational to ensuring that children's online experiences are positive and enriching. Here are some practical steps parents can take:

1. **Time Limits**: Implementing daily or weekly time limits on social media use helps prevent overconsumption and encourages children to engage in a variety of activities, both online and offline. Tools and apps that monitor usage can support these boundaries, making children more mindful of their screen time.

2. **Age-Appropriate Platforms**: Familiarize yourself with the platforms your child is interested in and ensure they are age-appropriate. Many social media platforms have age restrictions for a reason; respecting these guidelines can protect young users from content and interactions unsuitable for their age group.

3. **Digital Curfews**: Establishing times when devices should be turned off, especially around bedtime, can help ensure that social media use does not interfere with sleep or other critical restorative activities.

Critical Consumption of Online Content

In an age where information is abundant and not consistently accurate, teaching children to assess online content critically is essential. Here's how to cultivate discernment:

1. **Question Reliability**: Encourage children to ask questions about the source and purpose of the information they find online. "Who created this content, and why?" "Is this source reliable?" Teaching them to look for corroborating sources or evidence can help them develop a healthy skepticism.

2. **Understand Bias**: Discuss how online content can be biased and the importance of considering multiple viewpoints before forming an opinion. Highlight the value of fact-checking and reputable sources in navigating contentious or complex topics.

3. **Promote Media Literacy**: Engage in activities or use resources designed to improve media literacy. Understanding how media is made and the strategies used to capture attention or convey particular messages can arm children with the tools needed to navigate online content wisely.

Building a Kind Online Community

Creating and contributing to online communities characterized by kindness and positive interactions starts with intentional choices. Here's how families can cultivate such spaces:

1. **Choose Positive Spaces**: Research and select online platforms and communities known for their upbeat, supportive environments. Look for spaces with active moderation, clear community guidelines, and a culture aligning with your family's values.

2. **Lead by Example**: Demonstrate how to be a positive presence online by sharing uplifting content, engaging in respectful dialogue, and offering support or encouragement to others. Discuss these actions with your children, explaining why they matter and how they contribute to a kinder online community.

3. **Encourage Active Participation**: Motivate children to contribute positively to the online spaces they inhabit. This could mean creating content that reflects their interests and values, participating in campaigns or movements that promote kindness and inclusivity, or simply being a friendly, supportive voice in forums and discussions.

4. **Responding to Negativity**: Equip children with strategies for dealing with negative or unkind interactions online. Emphasize the importance of not engaging in harmful behaviors, using blocking and reporting features when necessary, and seeking support from adults when encountering troubling content or interactions.

By setting healthy boundaries, promoting critical content consumption, and actively contributing to kind online communities, parents and children can navigate the complexities of social media and online interactions in ways that are safe, enriching, and aligned with the values of empathy and respect. This guidance protects young users and empowers them to be agents of positive change in the digital world.

The Role of Parents in Digital Kindness

We'll conclude this chapter by highlighting the pivotal responsibilities that guardians bear in steering their children through the intricacies of the digital landscape with kindness and empathy at the forefront. This guidance is not just about preventing or avoiding the negatives but actively promoting a positive, compassionate online presence.

Ongoing Communication

The cornerstone of fostering digital kindness is maintaining open lines of communication between parents and children. This ongoing dialogue ensures that children feel comfortable sharing their online experiences, triumphs, and tribulations. Parents should regularly inquire, listen, and engage with their children about their digital lives, making it clear that no topic is off-limits and that curiosity is met with understanding, not judgment. This open communication fosters trust, making navigating discussions about online challenges and kindness opportunities easier.

Education about Digital Literacy

Equipping children with digital literacy tools is akin to teaching them how to navigate a map in unknown territories. It involves understanding the landscape (the internet and its platforms), recognizing the signs and symbols (identifying trustworthy sources and potential online risks), and knowing the language (communicating respectfully and understanding the impact of their words and actions online). Parents play a crucial role in this educational journey, providing resources, setting up learning opportunities, and sometimes learning alongside their children. This education is continuous, adapting to the ever-evolving digital sphere and its new challenges and opportunities for kindness.

Setting a Positive Example

Once again (here's that broken record!), the example they set is the most powerful tool at a parent's disposal. In an earlier chapter, we noted that children are astute observers, often mirroring the behaviors they see modeled by significant adults in their lives. By embodying the principles of digital kindness—through respectful online interactions, sharing positive content, and demonstrating empathy in digital communications—parents set a tangible standard for their children to follow. This modeling goes beyond telling children how to act; it shows them, in real-time, the impact of kindness in the digital realm.

The Journey Together

Fostering digital kindness is a journey parents and children embark on together. It requires patience, commitment, and a willingness to navigate the complexities of the digital world hand in hand. This path is marked by continuous learning and adapting strategies as children grow and the digital landscape shifts. It's a journey where successes are celebrated, mistakes are viewed as learning opportunities, and kindness is the guiding light.

The role of parents and caregivers in digital kindness cannot be overstated. Through ongoing communication, comprehensive education about digital literacy, and setting a positive example, parents can equip their children with the knowledge, skills, and values needed to navigate the digital world with kindness and empathy. This foundation enhances their children's online experiences and contributes to a broader culture of digital kindness, paving the way for a more compassionate online community for all.

Chapter 8:
Embracing Kindness as a Parent

We must be the change we wish to see in the world.
—Mahatma Gandhi

Parents wonder why the streams are bitter when they themselves have poisoned the fountain. —John Locke

To bring up a child in the way he should go, travel that way yourself once in a while. —Josh Billings

Self-Kindness in Parenting

In the quiet hours of early morning, before the sun had begun to erase the shadows of the night, Jordan found himself seated at the kitchen table, the remnants of yesterday's challenges lingering like the cold cup of coffee before him. As a parent, he had always set high standards for himself that seemed impossible on days like yesterday. The day had been a cascade of minor crises, from spilled breakfasts to missed appointments; each moment of frustration was met with an internal rebuke. "You should do better. You must do better," he would tell himself, the words a relentless echo in his mind.

It was in this moment of quiet reflection, however, that Jordan encountered a pivotal realization. The voice of self-criticism he believed was pushing him to be a better parent was draining the joy from parenting itself. It was a moment of clarity, sparked by the memory of his daughter's laughter as they pieced together a puzzle that evening—laughter that had momentarily lifted the weight of self-judgment. It dawned on Jordan that perhaps the path to being the parent he wanted to be didn't lie through harsh self-criticism but through kindness—kindness to himself.

Jordan's self-realization captures the essence of self-kindness in parenting. Self-kindness is not self-indulgence but a transformative approach that fosters compassion, empathy, and emotional resilience. It's about acknowledging that being a parent is a continuous learning journey, where mistakes are not failures but growth opportunities.

The psychological and emotional benefits of self-kindness are profound. For parents, practicing self-kindness can reduce stress, lower burnout risk, and improve emotional well-being. It promotes a healthier self-image and boosts confidence, influencing parenting behaviors. Parents who treat themselves with kindness are more likely to approach parenting challenges with patience and understanding, modeling these behaviors for their children.

Moreover, self-kindness fosters emotional resilience, providing parents with the inner resources needed to navigate the complexities of parenting. It encourages a mindset of growth and openness, allowing parents to respond to their children's needs with greater flexibility and compassion. This enhances the parent-child relationship and sets a powerful example for children, teaching them the value of kindness toward oneself and others.

In essence, self-kindness in parenting is about recognizing that to nurture kindness in our children, we must first extend it to ourselves. It is understanding that being kind to oneself is a foundational step in shaping a generation that values compassion and empathy. As parents journey toward incorporating more kindness into their lives, they not only enrich their own parenting experience but also impart invaluable lessons of love and compassion to their children.

Navigating Parenting Challenges

Navigating the multifaceted challenges of parenting requires deep reservoirs of patience, empathy, and kindness toward oneself and one's children. This dual application of kindness helps effectively address common parenting challenges and fosters an environment of understanding and compassion within the family. Here, we explore kindness-based strategies for managing some typical parenting hurdles.

When faced with a child's tantrum, the immediate impulse might be to respond with frustration or, conversely, to suppress one's feelings in an attempt to maintain calm. However, a kindness-based approach advocates for acknowledging one's emotional response while choosing to react with understanding toward the child. This involves taking a moment to breathe and recognizing that the tantrum is a form of communication, a child's way of expressing feelings they cannot yet articulate. Approaching the situation with empathy, trying to understand the underlying cause of the distress, and addressing it with patience can de-escalate the situation more effectively. It's equally important to acknowledge and be kind to oneself during these moments, recognizing that feeling overwhelmed is a natural response, not a failing.

Sibling rivalry presents another common challenge, often leaving parents feeling caught in the middle of constant bickering or competition. Addressing this issue with kindness involves first managing one's reactions to the rivalry, seeing it as an opportunity for teaching essential life skills like sharing, empathy, and negotiation rather than as a failure of sibling harmony. When discussing the issue, emphasize listening to each child's perspective without judgment, validating their feelings, and guiding them toward understanding each other's viewpoints. Demonstrating empathy and encouraging it in your children helps them learn to resolve conflicts more compassionately in the future.

Managing personal stress without falling into the trap of self-blame is crucial for maintaining the emotional well-being necessary for effective parenting. A kindness-based strategy for managing stress involves recognizing the signs of stress early and responding with self-care actions that address one's needs. This might include setting aside time for relaxation, pursuing hobbies, or seeking support from friends, family, or professionals. It's about treating oneself with the same compassion one would offer a friend in a similar situation, understanding that self-care is not selfish but essential for providing care for others.

Applying kindness internally and externally creates a nurturing environment where children learn to manage their emotions and interactions with empathy. It shows them that challenges can be met with understanding and compassion rather than frustration or indifference. For instance, a parent calmly explaining to a child that their feelings are valid but that there are more constructive ways to express them teaches the child emotional regulation through kindness. Similarly, guiding siblings to find a shared solution to a dispute demonstrates the value of empathy and cooperation.

In essence, navigating parenting challenges with kindness reinforces the idea that kindness is a strength. It offers practical solutions to everyday issues while also teaching invaluable life lessons. By modeling kindness in the face of challenges, parents address the immediate situation more effectively and lay the groundwork for their children to develop into compassionate, empathetic individuals.

Building a Kindness Community

While immensely rewarding, the parenting journey can also be isolating and challenging. In these moments, the support of a community that values kindness can be transformative. A "kindness community" among parents is more than just a support network; it's a collective that actively encourages and practices kindness within its ranks and beyond. This section explores how to connect with such communities and the myriad benefits they offer.

Connecting with like-minded parents can begin in your local neighborhood or extend globally through the power of the internet. Local parenting groups, often found through community centers, schools, or places of worship, provide a tangible sense of connection and the opportunity for face-to-face interaction. These groups can organize regular meet-ups, workshops, and family-friendly volunteer opportunities emphasizing kindness and community service.

In the digital realm, online forums and social media platforms are invaluable resources for finding and fostering a kindness community. Many platforms offer groups dedicated to parenting, where members share advice, experiences, and support. Look for groups that prioritize positive interactions and provide constructive feedback. Engaging in these online communities can extend your support network far beyond your immediate geographic location, offering diverse perspectives and a broader sense of belonging.

When seeking out or participating in these communities, consider the ethos of kindness in every interaction. Share your experiences and resources generously, offer support to those in need, and celebrate the successes of others with genuine enthusiasm. Contributing to the community not only aids others but also reinforces your commitment to kindness as a core parenting value.

The benefits of being part of a kindness community are manifold. Shared resources, from practical parenting tips to recommendations for books and activities that promote kindness, can be beneficial. Emotional support, particularly from those who have faced similar challenges, can offer comfort and reassurance during difficult times. Collective wisdom, aggregated experiences, and community knowledge can guide decision-making and inspire new approaches to common parenting dilemmas.

Moreover, belonging to a kindness community amplifies individual efforts to foster kindness. It creates a feedback loop where kindness begets kindness within the community and the wider world. As parents model kindness to their children, the community serves as an extended family that exemplifies these values, providing children with a broader context for understanding and practicing kindness.

In building or joining a kindness community, parents gain support for themselves and contribute to a more significant movement that champions kindness as a fundamental aspect of human interaction.

Illustrative Stories

In parenting, the journey toward self-kindness is both transformative and deeply impactful, not only for parents themselves but also for their children. It sets a foundation for a life viewed through the lens of compassion. Here, we explore narratives of parents and caregivers who've woven kindness into the fabric of their own lives, overcoming personal challenges and, in turn, enriching their family dynamics.

Julia's Journey to Self-Acceptance

Julia, a mother of three, struggled with the relentless pursuit of perfection in her parenting. This quest often left her feeling inadequate and overwhelmed, casting a shadow over the joy of raising her children. The turning point came when Julia began to attend a mindfulness group where the principle of self-kindness was emphasized. She learned to acknowledge her efforts and embrace her imperfections, realizing that her quest for perfection was an impossible and unnecessary burden.

This shift in perspective allowed Julia to view her parenting missteps not as failures but as opportunities for growth and connection with her children. She started to share her challenges openly with her kids, discussing the lessons learned and showing them that it's okay to be imperfect. This vulnerability led to a deeper, more authentic relationship with her children and taught them the value of self-compassion.

Marcus: Finding Balance in Single Parenthood

Marcus, raising his daughter alone, often found himself stretched thin between work demands, household responsibilities, and parenting. The pressure to be both mother and father to his daughter weighed heavily on him, leading to burnout and self-criticism. Marcus's perspective began to change when a fellow single parent introduced him to the concept of "kindness breaks" — short, intentional periods of self-care and reflection.

Incorporating these breaks into his daily routine, Marcus found that he could approach parenting challenges with more patience and clarity. By being kind to himself, he was better equipped to meet his daughter's needs with understanding and love. This practice of self-kindness both improved his well-being and modeled for his daughter the importance of taking care of oneself.

Emma's Transformation Through Gratitude

Emma, a parent navigating the complexities of raising a child with special needs, often felt isolated and overwhelmed by the challenges she faced—the constant focus on what was lacking led to a cycle of negativity and self-criticism. Everything changed when Emma began to practice gratitude, intentionally focusing on the daily joys and victories, no matter how small.

Despite its challenges, this gratitude practice opened Emma's eyes to the abundance of love and happiness in her life. It taught her to be kinder to herself, acknowledging the incredible strength and resilience she possessed. This newfound self-kindness radiated through her family, creating an atmosphere of positivity and resilience that uplifted everyone, especially her child.

The Power of Self-Kindness in Parenting

These stories from Julia, Marcus, and Emma highlight the profound impact that self-kindness can have on a parent's life and, by extension, their family. Embracing kindness toward oneself is not just an act of self-care; it's a powerful tool for personal transformation and shaping a nurturing, compassionate family environment. These narratives serve as motivational examples, illustrating that, despite the challenges, fostering a kindness mindset toward oneself is feasible and deeply rewarding. Through self-acceptance, balance, and gratitude, parents can navigate the complexities of parenting with grace, setting a loving example for the next generation.

Practical Tips

Integrating self-kindness into the rhythm of daily life is a practice that benefits not just individual parents but also their families, creating an environment where kindness becomes the norm. Building on the illustrative stories shared above, this section offers practical tips for embedding self-kindness and extending that compassion toward others. Here are some actionable strategies to consider:

1. **Set Aside Time for Self-Care**: Schedule regular, non-negotiable time for activities that rejuvenate your spirit and body. Whether it's reading, exercising, meditating, or pursuing a hobby, these moments of self-care are essential for maintaining your well-being and ability to extend kindness to others.

2. **Join a Supportive Community Group**: Connect with local or online groups that share your interests or parenting challenges. These communities offer a space for sharing experiences, providing and receiving support, and reminding you that you're not alone in your journey.

3. **Practice Daily Gratitude**: Start or end each day by listing three things you're grateful for. This simple practice shifts focus from what's lacking to the abundance in your life, fostering a mindset of appreciation and kindness toward oneself and one's circumstances.

4. **Employ Empathy Toward Yourself**: Treat yourself with the same empathy and understanding you would offer a friend when facing parenting challenges or personal setbacks. Speak to yourself compassionately, acknowledging your efforts and the intentions behind your actions.

5. **Learn to Say No**: Recognize your limits and feel comfortable setting boundaries. Saying no to additional responsibilities or engagements that stretch you too thin is an act of kindness toward yourself, allowing you to focus on your well-being and the things that truly matter.

6. **Celebrate Small Wins**: Acknowledge and celebrate your accomplishments, no matter how small. This recognition serves as a reminder of your strengths and contributions, reinforcing a positive self-image and encouraging continued acts of kindness toward yourself and others.

7. **Mindfulness and Meditation**: Incorporate mindfulness or meditation into your routine to foster a calm and compassionate inner dialogue. These practices can help you remain present, reduce stress, and approach situations with a more transparent, kinder perspective.

8. **Create a Kindness Journal**: Keep a journal dedicated to acts of kindness—both given and received—and moments of self-kindness. Reflecting on these entries can be a powerful reminder of the impact of kindness on your life and those around you.

9. **Model Kindness for Your Children**: Let your children see you practicing self-kindness and

extending kindness to others. Your actions teach them the value of compassion and how to apply it in their own lives.

10. **Seek Professional Support When Needed**: If you struggle to practice self-kindness or cope with parenting challenges, consider seeking support from a mental health professional. Sometimes, the kindest thing you can do for yourself is to reach out for help.

By adopting these practices, parents can cultivate a more profound sense of self-kindness and empathy, which inevitably spills over into their interactions with their children and others. Embracing self-care, connecting with supportive communities, and practicing daily gratitude are just a few ways to nurture a kindness mindset that transforms personal well-being and the familial and social fabric surrounding us.

Reflective Conclusion

As we draw this chapter to a close, let's pause and reflect on our journey together. This exploration of self-kindness and empathy has illuminated the profound impact that these practices can have on our well-being as parents and caregivers. In embracing kindness toward ourselves, we pave the way for a family life filled with understanding, patience, and love. Let these reflective prompts guide you in considering how fostering increased kindness toward yourself could transform your family dynamics:

1. **How does the way I treat myself influence my interactions with my family?** Reflect on moments when self-criticism or lack of self-kindness may have spilled into your family interactions. Consider how changing this internal dialogue to one of compassion and understanding could improve these interactions.

2. **How could increased self-kindness strengthen my relationships with my children or spouse?** Think about the model of empathy and compassion you wish to be for your family. How might your practice of self-kindness teach your children and demonstrate to your spouse the value of treating oneself and others with gentleness and respect?

3. **How might a more loving and forgiving approach to myself foster a more nurturing home environment?** Imagine the impact on your home's atmosphere if you were to regularly practice self-kindness and extend grace to yourself in moments of challenge or stress. Consider how this practice could create a ripple effect, encouraging all family members to adopt a similar stance of kindness and understanding.

In moving forward, remember to approach your journey toward self-kindness with warmth and grace. It's crucial to recognize this: the path to integrating self-kindness into your parenting ethos is not marked by perfection but by progress. Each step you take toward treating yourself with the same compassion you offer your children is a victory worth celebrating.

Embrace the understanding that there will be days when kindness toward oneself feels challenging, and that's okay. Remember, these moments do not signify failure but opportunities for growth and deeper self-compassion. Give yourself plenty of grace as you navigate the complexities of parenting and life. The kindness you cultivate within will enrich your life and set the stage for love and understanding within your loved ones, nurturing a home environment where kindness is the foundation of every interaction.

How thrilling it is to think about your efforts to embrace kindness toward yourself, which has the potential to create a legacy of love, empathy, and compassion that will resonate through your family for generations to come!

Chapter 9:
Kindness for Life

If I find in myself a desire which no experience in this world can satisfy, the most probable explanation is that I was made for another world. –C.S. Lewis, Mere Christianity

Carry out a random act of kindness with no expectation of reward, safe in the knowledge that one day, someone might do the same for you. –Princess Diana

A single act of kindness throws out roots in all directions, and the roots spring up and make new trees. –Amelia Earhart

Kindness That Lasts a Lifetime

In the heart of a small, bustling town nestled between rolling hills and whispering streams, there lived a man known to all as Grandfather Thomas. He was known not for wealth or status but for an act of kindness so simple yet profound that it would ripple across generations, becoming a cherished legacy within his family and the wider community.

The story begins during a particularly harsh winter in the early 20th century. The town, blanketed in snow, faced scarcities that tested the spirits of its inhabitants. Grandfather Thomas, then a young man, noticed a family new to town struggling more than most during this time. Without hesitation, he took it upon himself to anonymously leave baskets of food at their doorstep each week. This simple, thoughtful gesture of kindness provided sustenance and hope to a family on the brink of despair.

This act, small in execution but vast in heart, became the seed of kindness that Thomas would continue to sow throughout his life. But its story didn't end with him. As the years passed, this narrative of compassion and generosity was passed down through the generations, told and retold at family gatherings, becoming a foundational mythos for the family. Inspired by Grandfather Thomas's example, each descendant found ways to embody and pass on this legacy of kindness, embedding it deeply into their family values.

His daughter, inspired by the tales of her father's generosity, became a teacher who dedicated her life to nurturing and advocating for underprivileged children in her community. She taught her students the importance of compassion, often recounting her father's acts as examples, thus extending the roots of kindness beyond her family and into the hearts of countless children.

Years later, her own son, reflecting on his mother's stories and his grandfather's legacy, initiated a community garden. This garden wasn't just a food source; it was a place where people from all walks of life could come together, share stories, and support one another. The garden became a community hub, a testament to the enduring power of a single act of kindness.

As the family grew, so did the manifestations of Grandfather Thomas's original gesture. Inspired by his legacy, each act of kindness wove a richer tapestry of compassion and community spirit. His great-granddaughter, in a world now digital and fast-paced, carried this legacy into the online realm. She created a platform for sharing stories of kindness, a space that celebrated the goodness in humanity and inspired acts of kindness around the globe.

Grandfather Thomas's simple act of leaving food on a doorstep echoed through time, touching lives in ways he could never have imagined. It taught his descendants that kindness carries immense power, no matter how small it seems. It transcends time, transforming the immediate recipient and those who witness or hear about it, creating a ripple effect that can span generations.

This story reminds us that today's actions can become tomorrow's heritage. A single gesture of kindness can become a guiding light for generations. Kindness isn't just an act but can become a legacy, transcending time and becoming deeply embedded in the fabric of families and communities.

By embodying this spirit of kindness, we honor those who came before us and lay a foundation of compassion and empathy for those who follow.

I pray that each of us seeks to leave a legacy of the enduring power of kindness—a power that each of us holds, ready to be unleashed to shape a kinder, more compassionate world for generations to come.

Kindness For All of Life

Tales from around the globe illustrate the transformative power of kindness in various spheres of life. Acts of kindness can profoundly impact every sector of society, creating positive change, fostering unity, and enhancing well-being.

Schools: The Lunchtime Hero

In a US Midwest middle school, a lunch lady noticed a student consistently coming to school without a lunch and quietly sitting alone. Recognizing the signs of food insecurity and social isolation, she packed an extra lunch daily, leaving it anonymously for the student. Her act of kindness did not go unnoticed; it sparked a school-wide initiative where students and staff contributed to a fund ensuring no child went hungry. The initiative addressed immediate needs and fostered a culture of inclusivity and care, transforming the school into a community where every student felt valued and supported.

Workplaces: The Compassionate CEO

In a bustling tech startup in Bangalore, India, the CEO discovered that one of his employees was struggling with severe depression, impacting their work and personal life. Instead of reprimanding or dismissing the employee, the CEO offered support, including flexible working hours and resources for mental health care. This act of understanding and compassion helped the employee recover and set a new standard for the company. The CEO's kindness led to implementing a comprehensive wellness program, boosting morale and productivity and creating a workplace environment where employees felt genuinely cared for.

Communities: The Neighborhood's Heart

After a devastating hurricane hit a small coastal town in the Philippines, a local fisherman, despite losing his own home, focused on helping his neighbors. Using his boat, he rescued stranded families, distributed food and water, and organized shelter. His selfless actions inspired the community to unite, rebuilding homes and lives with renewed unity and resilience. The fisherman's kindness catalyzed a stronger, more cohesive community, demonstrating how bravery and compassion can turn tragedy into hope.

Politics: The Diplomat of Peace

In a time of political tension and unrest in a South American country, a young diplomat used her platform to bridge divides. She organized peace talks and community dialogues, focusing on shared human values rather than differences. Her efforts to understand and empathize with all sides led to ground-breaking agreements, reducing violence and opening paths to reconciliation. The diplomat's kindness and determination to see the humanity in everyone transformed political adversaries into partners for peace, proving that empathy can be a powerful tool in resolving conflicts.

Between Strangers: The Chain of Coffees

In a small cafe in Dublin, a customer decided to pay for the coffee of the person in line behind them, leaving a simple note: "Kindness is free. Sprinkle it everywhere." This small gesture sparked a chain reaction that lasted for days, with each recipient choosing to pay for the next person's order. The cafe became a local sensation, not just for its coffee but as a symbol of goodwill and community spirit. This story of kindness among strangers captured hearts globally, highlighting how a simple act can inspire a wave of generosity, bringing joy and connection to people's lives.

Healthcare: The Generous Pharmacist

In a bustling town in Italy, a pharmacist noticed an elderly customer hesitating over her prescription due to its cost. He quietly waived the fee without drawing attention, ensuring she received her medication. Moved by this act, the community began a fund to help those struggling to afford their prescriptions, managed by the pharmacy. This initiative provided vital medication to those in need and fostered a sense of solidarity and care within the community, transforming the pharmacy into a beacon of hope and support.

Sports: The Compassionate Coach

After a devastating loss that eliminated his team from a high school soccer tournament in Japan, a coach gathered his players not to critique but to praise their effort, teamwork, and sportsmanship. Recognizing the emotional toll, he organized team-building activities focused on mental health and resilience. This approach helped the team recover from their loss and built a stronger, more supportive squad. The coach's kindness in focusing on well-being over winning inspired other schools to adopt similar programs, highlighting the importance of emotional support in youth sports.

Arts and Culture: The Mural of Unity

In a divided neighborhood in South Africa, a local artist enlisted children to help paint a mural depicting scenes of community and cooperation. This project beautified the area and united residents from diverse backgrounds, fostering dialogue and understanding. The mural became a symbol of unity, prompting more community-driven art projects. This act of kindness through art demonstrated how creativity can bridge divides, encourage communication, and strengthen communal bonds.

Environmental Conservation: The Kindness Grove

A conservationist in Canada initiated a project called "The Kindness Grove," where each tree planted was dedicated to acts of kindness performed or received. Participants shared their stories, which were recorded in a book in the grove. This initiative contributed to reforestation efforts and created a living testament to kindness, encouraging visitors to reflect on their actions and the environment. The grove became a cherished space for reflection, education, and inspiration, showcasing the interconnectedness of kindness and environmental stewardship.

Public Services: The Library of Hope

In a small town in Australia, the local library started a "Book of Hope" project, where community members could write messages of encouragement, advice, and support. This book became a resource for those seeking comfort or guidance, growing into a community-wide movement of sharing and caring. Recognizing the project's impact, the library expanded its services to include workshops on empathy, mental health, and community support, reinforcing its role as a hub of kindness and a source of communal strength.

Kindness is a potent force for good, inspiring change and enriching lives in countless ways.

I had fun coming up with these fictional examples above to inspire and illustrate how kindness could manifest in various contexts globally; they're not based on specific real-life events or individuals. However, similar acts of kindness happen daily and are featured in news outlets, blogs, and social media platforms dedicated to positive news and storytelling. For authentic stories of kindness and their sources, I recommend at the end of the book a list of reputable sites that specialize in uplifting content. These platforms often highlight real-world instances of kindness across various sectors, providing inspiration and proof of the kindness in communities worldwide.

The Ripple Effect Revisited

At the heart of kindness lies a robust, almost magical quality: its ability to inspire further acts of kindness, creating a ripple effect that extends far beyond the initial gesture. We've noticed several times that this phenomenon, rooted in the basic human need for connection and empathy, is not just a feel-good theory but a social dynamic with the power to transform communities and societies.

Remember our earlier metaphor of a pebble thrown into a still pond—representing an act of kindness—dropped into a vast body of water? Ripples emanate outward from the point of impact, each wave reaching farther than the last. This visual metaphor embodies the essence of the ripple effect in social interactions. No matter how small, a single act of kindness can inspire subsequent acts of kindness. These, in turn, motivate others, creating an ever-widening circle of positive impact.

From the Individual to the World: The Expanding Circles of Kindness

1. **Individual Impact**: The immediate beneficiary of kindness experiences feelings of gratitude and upliftment, often leading to an increased desire to "pay it forward." This can be as simple as smiling at a stranger, mirroring the warmth received.

2. **Social Networks**: As individuals carry forward their acts of kindness, their social networks—friends, family, co-workers—observe and are often inspired to engage in their acts of kindness. This stage is crucial, as it marks the transition of kindness from a personal practice to a community value.

3. **Community Engagement**: Acts of kindness within a community, such as establishing a community garden or a collective art project, foster a sense of belonging and shared purpose. Community-level kindness initiatives can significantly enhance social cohesion and collective well-being.

4. **Societal Change**: When communities prioritize kindness, these values can influence broader societal norms and policies. Acts of kindness become embedded in cultural practices,

educational curricula, and even governance, leading to a society that values and promotes empathy and compassion.

A Personal Note

My belief in Jesus Christ's historical teachings and examples gives me the lens through which I look at all of this. However, like many Christians, I find it deeply unfortunate, frustrating, and glaring that so many of the seeds of division in the world today are sown by those in our faith family.

Let me illustrate this in the language of computers. For a Christian, kindness isn't merely a *software program*; kindness is our *operating system*. We don't open kindness when we need it to serve our purposes, and we close it when that purpose is done. Kindness is embedded deeply into how we run our lives—it's part of the foundation of all the processes of our lives. An unkind Christian is *incompatible* with a normative reading of the Bible. Why, then, does it seem like there are so many around us? Even the most faithful Christian might sometimes struggle to show kindness, especially when faced with stress, illness, tragedy, or trauma. However, in my experience, most followers of Jesus who aren't kind don't read the *operator's manual* very much and are likely to live their lives using *poorly written code* from errant faith leaders.

Analogy aside, the fact of the matter is this: kindness is one of the most basic tenets of the Christian faith. (It's included on the list referred to as the "fruit of the Spirit" in Galatians chapter five if you look it up.) I am among many Christians worldwide committed to personally and professionally living a kind life as conveyed in the pages of ancient scripture. Throughout this book, I haven't listed many specific passages from the Bible, but what I've written is based on what can be found on many of those precious pages.

Some of you will share this worldview; many of you won't. I hope and pray that I've done justice to our theme at hand and given you faithful, practical, and simple teaching on one of the traits for which a Christian should be most and best known.

Passing It On

We stand at a crossroads. The paths before us stretch into the future, each step marked by the choices we make and the values we uphold. We hold the power to shape the world we leave behind for generations. The journey through the pages of this book has been one of discovery, reflection, and, most importantly, action. It has been a call to recognize and embrace the profound impact of kindness—a potent force that can transform our lives and the world around us.

The narrative of kindness is as old as humanity itself, yet it remains our most renewable resource. In every act of kindness, we witness the ripple effect—a cascade of positive change initiated by a single gesture. Like that pebble tossed into the pond, each act of kindness, no matter how small, sends waves across the surface of our collective consciousness. These ripples touch lives, open hearts, and bring us closer, proving time and again that our capacity for compassion abounds.

We are called to be the pebble that initiates those ripples, understanding that our actions, imbued with kindness, have the potential to inspire, uplift, and unite. In a world that often prioritizes division over unity and self-interest over communal well-being, choosing kindness is both revolutionary and deeply healing. It is a statement of hope and goodness and a commitment to bringing that goodness to light.

Regardless of where you're coming from and where you'll go from here, consider the power of embodying and promoting kindness as you reflect on the legacy you wish to leave. Imagine a future where kindness is not an afterthought but the foundation of our interactions—where children grow up understanding the value of compassion, communities thrive on mutual respect, and societies are built on the principles of empathy and understanding. This vision is not beyond our reach; it begins with the choices we make today, the kindness we choose to give, and the kindness we teach our children to embrace.

Let us take up the mantle of kindness with determination and joy, knowing that each act of kindness, each moment of understanding, and each gesture of compassion adds to a legacy that transcends time. We are the architects of our future, and with kindness as our guide, we can build a world that reflects the best of who we are.

Our final rallying cry is not just a conclusion to the journey through a book but an invitation to carry forward the torch of kindness and to illuminate the path for others.

Let kindness be the balm that mends our divisions and brings us together in a world needing healing.

Dear reader, embrace kindness as a core life value, and watch as the world transforms around you—one act of kindness at a time.

Together, my friend, we can create a legacy of kindness that endures, inspiring generations and shaping a brighter, more compassionate future for everyone.

The world has too many critics.

We need more kindness.

Pass it on.

Appendix:
Resources for Furthering Kindness

Learning never exhausts the mind. –Leonardo da Vinci

Education is not preparation for life; education is life itself.
–John Dewey

Start with areas you feel most drawn to or areas where you seek more growth and understanding.

Books

Parenting and Kindness

These books provide valuable insights into parenting, focusing on nurturing kindness and empathy in children. They offer a comprehensive range of approaches and insights into how to raise children who are not only successful but also kind, empathetic, and emotionally intelligent. This selection includes both practical guides and theoretical works.

- "The Whole-Brain Child: 12 Revolutionary Strategies to Nurture Your Child's Developing Mind" by Daniel J. Siegel and Tina Payne Bryson offers practical strategies for developing a child's emotional intelligence and fostering empathetic relationships.

- "UnSelfie: Why Empathetic Kids Succeed in Our All-About-Me World" by Michele Borba explores the importance of empathy in child development and provides a step-by-step guide to teaching children to be empathetic.

- "Raising Good Humans: A Mindful Guide to Breaking the Cycle of Reactive Parenting and Raising Kind, Confident Kids" by Hunter Clarke-Fields and Carla Naumburg is a practical guide that offers mindful parenting techniques that foster kindness, compassion, and empathy.

- "How to Raise Kind Kids: And Get Respect, Gratitude, and a Happier Family in the Bargain" by Thomas Lickona delves into the practical aspects of raising respectful and considerate children in a compassionate family environment.

- "The Power of Showing Up: How Parental Presence Shapes Who Our Kids Become and How Their Brains Get Wired" by Daniel J. Siegel and Tina Payne Bryson explains how a parent's emotional presence contributes to a child's social and emotional development.

- "Roots of Empathy: Changing the World Child by Child" by Mary Gordon discusses a program that has proven effective in increasing children's empathy and emotional literacy worldwide.

- "Parenting from the Inside Out: How a Deeper Self-Understanding Can Help You Raise Children Who Thrive" by Daniel J. Siegel and Mary Hartzell explores the neurological aspects of parenting and how understanding one's brain can help raise kind and compassionate children.

- "Born for Love: Why Empathy Is Essential—and Endangered" by Maia Szalavitz and Bruce D. Perry examines empathy's critical role in human development and societal functioning and offers insights into how it can be nurtured from childhood.

Empathy and Compassion

Here's a list of books that dive into the science and philosophy of empathy and compassion, providing a deeper understanding of these essential aspects of human interaction. They offer a variety of perspectives and deep dives into understanding empathy and compassion not just as personal emotions but as forces that shape societies and interactions.

- "The Age of Empathy: Nature's Lessons for a Kinder Society" by Frans de Waal. De Waal draws on his extensive research with primates to argue that humans are naturally empathetic and cooperative, challenging the notion that society is built on self-interest.

- "The Art of Empathy: A Complete Guide to Life's Most Essential Skill" by Karla McLaren. This book explains how empathy works, why it's invaluable, and how to cultivate it to improve personal relationships and overall well-being.

- "Compassion and Conviction: The AND Campaign's Guide to Faithful Civic Engagement" by Justin Giboney, Michael Wear, and Chris Butler. From a Christian perspective, this book guides how to approach politics and civic responsibilities with compassion and empathy, integrating faith into these areas without compromising core values.

- "Mere Christianity" by C.S. Lewis is a seminal work in Christian apologetics. It offers a rational basis for Christianity and a profound exploration of morality, including the role of love, empathy, and compassion in the Christian life.

Personal Development

Here's a list of books encouraging personal growth and the development of kindness and emotional intelligence in adults. These books offer psychological insights, practical advice, and spiritual wisdom to help adults foster personal growth and develop greater kindness and emotional intelligence.

- "Emotional Intelligence: Why It Can Matter More Than IQ" by Daniel Goleman. Goleman's groundbreaking book discusses the importance of emotional intelligence in success and personal happiness and offers strategies for developing empathy, self-awareness, and interpersonal skills.

- "The Book of Joy: Lasting Happiness in a Changing World" by the Dalai Lama, Desmond Tutu, and Douglas Abrams captures conversations between the Dalai Lama and Archbishop Desmond Tutu. The book explores themes of joy, suffering, and compassion and emphasizes the power of kindness.

- "Everybody, Always: Becoming Love in a World Full of Setbacks and Difficult People" by Bob Goff combines Christian teachings with real-life stories to inspire readers to practice love and acceptance in everyday encounters. The book emphasizes that love and kindness should extend to everyone, always.

- "Dare to Lead: Brave Work. Tough Conversations. Whole Hearts." by Brené Brown discusses the role of vulnerability in leadership, encouraging readers to lead with empathy, connection, and courage—qualities essential for personal growth and effective leadership.

Websites and Online Resources

Here's a list of websites, online platforms, and blogs that provide resources, tips, and communities focused on parenting with kindness, including those with a strong foundation in promoting kindness and empathy from various perspectives. These platforms offer a variety of tools and perspectives on raising kind, empathetic children, catering to a broad audience of parents looking to cultivate these qualities in their families.

- The Greater Good Science Center (https://greatergood.berkeley.edu/).
  This website offers many resources and articles on the science of a meaningful life, including sections dedicated to family and parenting. It provides research-based strategies for fostering kindness and empathy in children.

- Aha! Parenting (http://www.ahaparenting.com/). Dr. Laura Markham's site offers advice, tips, and effective parenting strategies centered on empathy and peaceful parenting approaches.

- Hand in Hand Parenting (https://www.handinhandparenting.org/). This site provides tools and support for parents to address their children's behavior challenges with compassion and empathy, promoting closer emotional bonds.

- Focus on the Family (https://www.focusonthefamily.com/) is an organization that guides families and parenting. It offers resources for nurturing kindness and empathy within a Christian values framework.

- Doing Good Together (http://www.doinggoodtogether.org/). This organization strongly focuses on family volunteering and offers numerous ideas on how parents can engage children in acts of kindness and community service, thereby teaching empathy through action.

- Kindness.org (https://www.kindness.org/) is a platform that encourages people to participate in acts of kindness and share their experiences. It offers educational resources that focus on fostering kindness in schools and communities, including initiatives for parents and educators.

About the Author

Charlie Lyons has dedicated over 20 years to non-profit and local church leadership, serving as a youth leader, children's program leader, pastor, missionary, and chaplain. As a parent of three children, ranging from tweens to teens, Charlie draws from personal and professional experience to offer practical, heartfelt guidance to other parents navigating the complexities of raising kind and compassionate children.

Kindness For Life is Charlie's debut book, authored out of his deep-seated belief in the transformative power of kindness. Recognized by those he serves as one of the kindest people they know, Charlie is passionate about fostering environments where empathy and compassion can thrive. His work as a chaplain has further honed his understanding of kindness's profound impact on individuals and communities. He believes in the power of shared experiences and mutual support among parents.

His commitment to kindness is a professional endeavor and a personal mission that lights up his life. Few things bring Charlie more joy than guiding and nurturing his children to become kind-hearted individuals.

Charlie, his wife Lindsey, and their three children reside in Brantford, Ontario.

References

Bandura, A. (1969). Social-learning theory of identificatory processes. In D. A. Goslin (Ed.), *Handbook of socialization theory and research* (pp. 213-262). Rand McNally & Company. Available at https://www.academia.edu/download/43540100/Bandura1969HSTR.pdf

Fritz, M. (2019). Kindness and cellular aging: A pre-registered experiment testing the effects of prosocial behavior on telomere length and well-being. Retrieved from https://scholar.archive.org/work/owrzjlbjlvb6pc4kod7ta6bjqq/access/wayback/https://escholarship.org/content/qt9t81j2hj/qt9t81j2hj.pdf?t=pv3c7s

Iacoboni, M. (2009). Imitation, Empathy, and Mirror Neurons. Annual Review of Psychology, 60, 653-670. https://www.annualreviews.org/content/journals/10.1146/annurev.psych.60.110707.163604

Kumar, S. A., Edwards, M. E., Grandgenett, H., & Simons-Rudolph, J. (2022). Does gratitude promote resilience during a pandemic? An examination of mental health and positivity at the onset of COVID-19. *Journal of Happiness*

Studies. https://doi.org/10.1007/s10902-022-00554-x

Layous, K., Nelson, S. K., Kurtz, J. L., & Lyubomirsky, S. (2017). What triggers prosocial effort? A positive feedback loop between positive activities, kindness, and well-being. *The Journal of Positive Psychology*, *12*(4), 385–398. https://doi.org/10.1080/17439760.2016.1198924

Lutz, A., Brefczynski-Lewis, J., Johnstone, T., & Davidson, R. J. (2008). Regulation of the neural circuitry of emotion by compassion meditation: effects of meditative expertise. *PLoS One, 3*(3), e1897. https://doi.org/10.1371/journal.pone.0001897

Malik, F., & Shujja, S. (2013). Emotional intelligence and academic achievement: Implications for children's performance in schools. *Journal of the Indian Academy of Applied Psychology, 39*(1), 37-45. Available at https://www.researchgate.net/publication/287320527_Emotional_intelligence_and_academic_achievement_Implications_for_children's_performance_in_schools

Paavola, L. E. (2017). The importance of emotional intelligence in early childhood. [PDF file].

Retrieved from https://www.theseus.fi/bitstream/handle/10024/131619/BA%20Thesis%20of%20Lilla%20Paavola.pdf?sequence

Post, S. G. (2011). It's good to be good: 2011 fifth annual scientific report on health, happiness, and helping others. *International Journal of Person Centered Medicine, 1*(2), 249-259. Available at http://www.ijpcm.org/index.php/IJPCM/article/view/154

Schokman, C., Downey, L. A., Lomas, J., Wellham, D., Wheaton, A., & Simmons, N. (2014). Emotional intelligence, victimisation, bullying behaviours and attitudes. *Learning and Individual Differences, 37*, 193-200. https://doi.org/10.1016/j.lindif.2014.11.024

Shobitha, M., & Kohli, S. K. (2015). Physiological effects of practice of loving-kindness meditation. *Int. J. Physiol., 3*(1), 1-5. Retrieved from https://www.researchgate.net/publication/273507030_Brainstem_Auditory_Evoked_Potential_Changes_in_Iron_Deficient_Anaemic_Children

Tomczyk, J., Nezlek, J. B., & Krejtz, I. (2022). Gratitude can help women at-risk for depression accept their depressive symptoms, which leads to improved mental health. *Frontiers in Psychology, 13*,

Article 878819. https://doi.org/10.3389/fpsyg.2022.878819

Wood, A. M., Froh, J. J., & Geraghty, A. W. A. (2010). Gratitude and well-being: A review and theoretical integration. *Clinical Psychology Review, 30*(7), 890-905. https://doi.org/10.1016/j.cpr.2010.03.005

Manufactured by Amazon.ca
Acheson, AB